Sounds of the Soul

LIAN HUSI KLAMAR

For Yolan, Milena & Di

Thank you so much for your
tireless work on the translation of
sounds of the soul – Lian thoi/Klamer
and solidarity throughout!
with Love & Affection

Ros xx

LIAN HUSI KLAMAR

MÚSIKA TRADISIONÁL HUSI TIMOR-LESTE

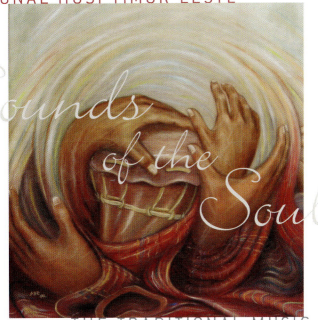

Sounds
of the
Soul

THE TRADITIONAL MUSIC OF EAST TIMOR

Ros Dunlop

Richard Daschbach kontribui ba kapítulu kona-ba Oekusi
Contribution for the Oekusi chapter by Richard Daschbach

TEKEE MEDIA

Roslyn Dunlop
Lian Husi Klamar : Músika Tradisionál Husi Timor-Leste
Sounds of the Soul : The Traditional Music of East Timor

Published by Tekee Media Inc
17 Callan Street
Rozelle NSW 2039 Australia
www.tekeemedia.com

This book was made possibe with the generous
support of the United States Embassy in Dili, through
the United States Department of State.

ISBN 978-0-646-58183-5

Tetun Editors : Jonathan York and Milena da Silva
English Editor : Susan Shineberg
Designer : Penelope Lee
Printer : Prolong Press, China

To the people of East Timor

Dedika ba povu Timor

Contents
TABELA KONTEÚDU

Lia Maklokek	ix
Agradesimentu	xii
Terminolojia	xvi
Mapa Distritál ba Instrumentu Tradisionál Sira	xviii

INTRODUSAUN — 21

MÚZIKA TRADISIONÁL DANSA NIAN — 27

Introdusaun	28
Roupa Tradisionál	31
dahur	32
tebedai	33
likurai	34
bidu	35

Dansa Ne'ebé Aprezenta Ai-Knanoik	39
makikit	39
maulelo	39

Instrumentu Sira Ne'ebe Akompaña Dansa	43
baba	43
baba dook	43
baba dook ki'ik	44
tala	44
ailoos	44
raraun	45
lakadou	50

MÚZIKA TRADISIONÁL OEKUSI NIAN — 55

Introdusaun	57
takanab	58
bsoot and lelan	63
bano	64
ke'e	68
sene	68
bonet	70
bonet sit ualu	74
muiskatele	74
oebani	74
pankalalále	75

Nel Lima	79
nel número ida	80
nel número rua	81
nel número tolu	82
nel número haat	82
nel número lima	83

INSTRUMENTU RITUAL — 85

karau dikur	88
kokotere	88
tohin	92
tihak	94
titir	95
bobakasa/tambor	96
popokasa	96

INSTRUMENTU SIRA IHA MORIS LOROLORON — 103

Introdusaun	105
kakal'uta	106
kakalo	107
fiku no ka pai koe-koe	107
kafu'i	110
lesun no alu	111
rama	114
kakeit	116
bijol meto	117
au	121

KNANANUK TRADISIONÁL — 123

Introdusaun	125
Knananuk ho Dansa	128
Knananuk Ritual Nian	132
Knananuk Moris Loroloron Nian	142
Knananuk ho Lakadou	148

Glosáriu	152
Notas	156
Lista Livru Sira	158
Kréditu ba Fotografia husi Pintura Sira	159

Preface	x
Acknowledgements	xiv
Nomenclature	xvi
District Map of Traditional Instruments	xviii

INTRODUCTION — 24

TRADITIONAL MUSIC OF DANCE — 27
Introduction	29
Traditional Dress	31
dahur	36
tebedai	36
likurai	37
bidu	37

Dances That Tell a Story	40
makikit	40
maulelo	41

Instruments Accompanying Dance	43
baba	47
baba dook	47
baba dook ki'ik	48
tala	48
ailoos	49
raraun	49
lakadou	52

TRADITIONAL MUSIC OF OEKUSI — 55
Introduction	57
takanab	60
bsoot and lelan	66
bano	67
ke'e	69
sene	69
bonet	72
eight bonet sit	76
muiskatele	76
oebani	76
pankalalále	76

Five Nels	79
nel one	80
nel two	81
nel three	82
nel four	82
nel five	83

TRADITIONAL MUSIC OF RITUAL — 85
Introduction	87
karau dikur	90
kokotere	90
tohin	98
tihak	99
titir	101
bobakasa/tambor	101
popokasa	101

TRADITIONAL MUSIC OF DAILY LIFE — 103
Introduction	105
kakalo	108
fiku or ka pai koe-koe	108
kakal'uta	109
kafu'i	112
lesun no alu	113
rama	114
kakeit	118
bijol meto	119
au	121

TRADITIONAL SONG — 123
Introduction	126
Songs of Dance	128
Songs of Ritual	132
Songs of Daily Life	142
Songs with Lakadou	148

Glossary	154
Notes	156
Reading and Listening Sources	158
Picture Credits	159

LIA MAKLOKEK

Bainhira ha'u hetan oferta atu bá vizita Timor-Leste ho Robert no Martin Wesley-Smith iha tinan 2002, ha'u nunka imajina oinsá viajen ne'e sei halo impaktu boot ba ha'u-nia moris. Agora tinan sanulu depois, ha'u sei bá-mai hela, hadomi no admira nafatin rai Timor ho ninia ema no sira-nia kultura, liuliu sira-nia múzika tradisionál.

Robert Wesley-Smith hanesan ativista ida ne'ebé suporta Timor-Leste nia hakarak ba ukun rasik an horikedas tinan 1975. Nia husu ninia alin mane, Martin, kompozitór no ativista, no ha'u (klarinetista ida) atu akompaña nia bá Timor atu toka iha konsertu balu, husi múzika ne'ebé Martin rasik mak hakerek. Múzika ne'e ho tema kona-ba tempu okupasaun Indonézia iha Timor-Leste. Bainhira ami sa'e aviaun semo mai Timor, ami la hatene saida loos mak ami sei hetan iha Timor. Iha tempu ne'ebá ema hotu akompaña hela prosesu kampaña ba eleisaun prezidensiál ba dahuluk iha nasaun foun ida ne'e. Ami mós sente entuziazmu boot iha momentu ne'ebá, no ami mós laran monu kedas ba Timor-Leste nia povu no kultura.

Bainhira ami halo lemo-rai ba distritu balu, ami nota katak ema barak toka múzika espontánea iha fatin barak. Ami haree ema la'o iha estrada ninin, toka instrumentu no kanta hela. Ami hanoin buat hanesan ne'e kapás loos. Ami bá fatin barak hodi hatudu konsertu no ami lori ekipamentu eletróniku barak uitoan. Iha knua rua, katuas balu dehan katak presiza grava hodi rai sira-nia múzika ba jerasaun sira tuir mai. Sira ta'uk katak múzika tradisionál sei mate bainhira sira mate. Ha'u observa katak ikus mai ne'e, ema ladún toka múzika espontánea barak hanesan uluk.

Hafoin ha'u-nia viajen primeira, ha'u sente katak ha'u hakarak fó fali kontribuisaun ruma, tanba ha'u sente riku ho esperiénsia kona-ba buat hotu ne'ebé ha'u rona no haree iha Timor. Nune'e depois viajen ne'e, ha'u mai filafali ba tempu barak nia laran atu halo gravasaun múzika tradisionál. Buat ne'e só bele halo tanba Timoroan barak mak ajuda. Dahuluk, múziku sira hakarak no sente importante atu rai sira-nia múzika ba jerasaun sira iha futuru mai. Daruak, Timoroan sira ne'ebé ajuda ha'u, dala barak joven sira ne'e mai husi knua sira ne'ebé ami atu tun ba halo gravasaun. Sira maka fasilita buat hotu para gravasaun bele akontese duni. Joven sira ne'e mai husi eskola *Arte Moris* no *Centro Archivo Max Stahl Timor-Leste* komprende importánsia atu halo gravasaun sira ne'e. Karik lahó sira-nia ajuda, projetu ne'e labele la'o.

When I was offered the opportunity to travel to East Timor with Robert and Martin Wesley-Smith in April 2002, I never imagined the affect that journey would have on my life. Here I am ten years later, still travelling to and from East Timor, as enchanted by the country, the people and their culture, in particular their traditional music, as I was on that first trip.

Robert Wesley-Smith, a long time activist and staunch supporter of East Timor, suggested to his brother Martin, composer and activist, and myself, a classical musician (clarinettist) that we accompany him to East Timor to give some concerts of the music Martin had written for audiovisuals and clarinet. These compositions were about the history of East Timor in the years of Indonesian occupation. We had no idea what to expect as we flew into Dili. The country was abuzz with the fervour leading up to the elections of the first president for the world's newest nation, East Timor. We were swept along in the excitement, and fell under the spell of the country, its people and its culture.

Travelling through the districts we observed that there was an abundance of spontaneous music-making. We saw people walking along the roads, playing instruments and singing. We thought it was wonderful. As we toured East Timor with the large amounts of electronic equipment needed for staging these concerts, some of the elders of a couple of villages remarked on the need to preserve their music for posterity. They were concerned that the traditional musical culture would die with their passing. I have observed in subsequent trips to East Timor how much spontaneous music-making has dwindled.

I left East Timor after that first trip feeling enriched by all that I saw and heard, wanting to give something in return. So began countless trips to East Timor recording the traditional music, recordings that would not have been possible without the help of so many Timorese. First, the wonderful musicians keen for their music to be preserved for successive generations, acutely aware of the importance of recording their music for posterity. Secondly, the Timorese who were my assistants. Mostly these young men and women would be from the village we were going to record in and organised the succession of events that allowed a recording to take place. The paintings throughout this book are all the work of the talented artists of *Arte Moris*. These young people and the young Timorese from the audiovisual archive, *Centro Archivo Max Stahl Timor-Leste*, understood the importance of a permanent record being made. Without their considerable help this project would not have happened.

AGRADESIMENTU

Ha'u fó obrigada ba múziku, artista, organizasaun sira no ema hotu ne'ebé maka fó kontribuisaun atu halo livru ne'e posivel.

Dahuluk, ba múziku Timoroan sira ne'ebé fahe sira-nia talentu no matenek ho laran luak. Sira komprende katak presiza halo dokumentasaun permanente ba sira-nia kultura muzikál. Obrigada espesiál ba Manuel Pereira no Pedro Tilman ne'ebé toka *lakadou*, hanesan múziku tradisionál primeiru ne'ebé ha'u koñese. Ho sira-nia gravasaun, projetu ne'e hahú la'o. Obrigada ba diretór sira husi grupu múzika tradisionál nian hotu, ne'ebé ajuda barak no loke dalan ba ha'u atu koñese sira-nia múzika.

Produsaun ba livru ne'e sei la sai realidade se kuandu la hetan tulun, fundus, no apoiu husi Embaixada Estadus Unidus Amerikanu nian iha Dili. Liuliu Sr. Hans Klemm, ex-Embaixadór EUA nian ba Timor-Leste, no Jonathan Henick no Januario Soares. Obrigada espesiál mós ba Tricia Johns, ne'ebé hatudu ha'u-nia DVD kona-ba múzika tradisionál ba Embaixadór Klemm, nune'e ami bele koñese malu.

Obrigada ba Sekretária Estadu Kultura, liuliu Sr. Virgilio Smith no Sr. Eugenio Sarmento ne'ebé fahe sira-nia matenek ba ha'u. Obrigada ba Lucas Serrao Lopes ne'ebé fó informasaun sobre serimónia ikan-pari. Obrigada mós ba Nuno Oliveira, ne'ebé hanorin ha'u buat barak, no obrigada mós ba Karen Myers ne'ebé sai hanesan ponte ligasaun entre ha'u ho Sekretária Estadu Kultura. Obrigadu boot mós ba Richard Daschbach ba ninia kontribuisaun kona-ba múzika Oekusi nian no fó koneksaun ba maluk Timoroan sira husi Oekusi. Obrigada ba Atilio da Costa husi Caritas Oekusi, ne'ebé ajuda ho informasaun sobre múzika, no mós Wade Freeman ne'ebé foti knaar boot ida nu'udar ponte hodi fó koneksaun entre ha'u no maluk Oekusi oan sira.

Obrigada ba alin artista sira hotu iha Arte Moris, no ba fundadór sira Gabi no Luca Gansser ne'ebé ajuda barak liu durante tinan barak nia laran bainhira ha'u mai halo peskiza no gravasaun iha Timor. Obrigada ba artista sira ne'ebé fó lisensa atu publika sai sira-nia arte furak sira iha livru ida ne'e. Liuliu ba Tony Amaral ne'ebé kontribui dezeñu ba livru labarik nian, ninia pintura sira, ninia pasiénsia, kómiku, no amizade durante lemo-rai barak iha Timor no mós durante serbisu to'o kalan boot barak iha Sydney bainhira halo tradusaun husi Tetun ba Inglés. Obrigada mós ba Pelle Pereira ne'ebé kontribui ilustrasaun ba livru labarik nian. Cesario Soares Lourdes, ne'ebé kontribui ilustrasaun, pasiénsia, diplomasia, no serbisu la kole bainhira serbisu iha kampu. Alfeo Sanches Pereira, ba ninia pintura, ninia hamnasa, ninia kanta no laran kmanek bainhira serbisu lemo-rai. Etson Caminha, Adilson Arintis da Costa Caminha, no Ananias Carlos ba knananuk iha lian Fataluku ne'ebé iha CD laran. Osme Gonçalves, ba ninia múzika Fataluku, tradusaun no istória sira. Lely Barreto ne'ebé halo gravasaun ba Osme nia múzika.

Knaar na'in hotu iha Centro Audio-Visual Max Stahl Timor-Leste ne'ebé ajuda durante viajen barak. Max Stahl, ba ninia amizade no konsellu ne'ebé sempre fó ba ha'u durante peskiza tinan barak nia laran, no ba ninia família ne'ebé simu ha'u ho laran midar no hamaluk ha'u durante ha'u-nia viajen barak mai Dili.

Abel Gutterres, ba ninia apoiu no amizade durante peskiza tinan barak. Gillian Howell, ba informasaun no konsellu, no ba ninia parseiru Tony Hicks ne'ebé fó lisensa atu uza ninia foto ida husi *kakalo*. Sejismundo Pedru Valentim Ray, peskizadór no fotógrafu ne'ebé ajuda ho transkrisaun múzika no instrumentu sira husi Ataúru. Ha'u apresia tebes tanba ami konsege halo lailais iha tempu ne'ebé badak.

Jose Trindade, tanba nia hanorin ha'u buat barak kona-ba ninia kultura. Ameta Jorges Ximenes Mendonça, ba ninia informasaun kona-ba múzika no kultura Makasae nian. Abilio dos Santos, tanba nia mak organiza demonstrasaun *kakal'uta* nian. Iliwatu (Julianto Pereira,) ba informasaun kona-ba *baba dook titir*, ne'ebé ita kuaze nunka haree.

Charline Bodin, ba lemo-rai kapás ida, no mós ba serbisu buka tuir informasaun sira ne'ebé sei falta bainhira prosesu hakerek livru ne'e besik atu remata. Justino Valentim, tanba nia editór ba testu iha lian Fataluku, no mós tanba nia fahe ninia matenek sobre instrumentu sira, múzika, no ai-knanoik husi kultura Fataluku. No mós tanba nia hanesan uma-na'in ne'ebé di'ak no hatene oinsá simu ninia bainaka sira. Melchior Dias Fernandes, ne'ebé lori karreta no troka roda dala barak, te'in etu, no fase bikan la para durante viajen ikus liu antes atu publika livru ne'e.

Susan Shineberg, ha'u-nia editór, ho ninia 'matan makikit' hodi hadi'a livru ne'e, no sempre suporta ha'u durante prosesu tomak. Obrigada boot ba Jonathan York no Milena da Silva ba imi nia matenek, laran-luak, no versaun Tetun ba livru ne'e. Vernon Tupper, Fiona Napier Flood, David Watson no Gail Clifford ne'ebé lee uluk livru ne'e hodi buka no hadi'a sala ne'ebé iha.

Kirsty Sword Gusmão, ne'ebé mós lee livru labarik nian no oferese sujestaun oinsá atu bele hadi'a di'ak liu tan. Ego Lemos, Luciano Malaisiku, James Laidler, Wendy no Michael Dixon, Ingrid Bucens ne'ebé mós fó idea kona-ba livru ba labarik nian. Obrigada barak ba imi hotu.

Elizabeth Adams ne'ebé lori todan tanba ha'u sempre obriga nia atu konfirma ba dala barak informasaun no matéria hotu, múzika, no konsellu ba livru labarik nian. Marqi da Costa, tanba nia mós uma-na'in ne'ebé di'ak no hatene oinsá atu simu nia bainaka sira bainhira ami halo peskiza. Marie Claire Sweeney, kolega di'ak ne'ebé sempre fó suporta no konsellu di'ak durante tinan barak nia laran dezde ami koñese malu iha Timor. Gail Clifford no Ceu Lopes Federer, ba sira-nia suporta durante etapa balu iha projetu laran. Maire Sheehan, nu'udar manu ain ne'ebé lori ilustrasaun husi Timor ba Austrália. Anne Finch ne'ebé fó konsellu di'ak. Jenni Kanaley ne'ebé loke ninia koleksaun tais, instrumentu sira, no livru sira, no mós ba ninia suporta boot.

Louise Byrne, ne'ebé hatutan ninia matenek no ninia teze mai ha'u. Patsy Thatcher ne'ebé sujere livru barak ba ha'u atu lee. Ron Reeves, Ida Lawrence no Peter Dunbar-Hall ba sira-nia ajuda ho sistema hakerek notas Indonézia nian. Jim Chapman no Richard Vella, ba sira-nia konsellu bainhira ha'u hakerek hela livru ne'e.

Rob no Martin Wesley-Smith ne'ebé merese atu hetan obrigada boot duni tanba sira mak fó idea mai ha'u atu mai vizita Timor-Leste ba dala primeira. To'o agora sira hanesan kolega di'ak liu ne'ebé sempre suporta ha'u. Ba Penelope no John Lee, ha'u hato'o obrigada ho laran tomak ba dezeñu kapás ba livru ida-ne'e. Harry Bennetts, ha'u-nia oan mane tanba nia mós ajuda lee no hadi'a testu sira, no mós ba ninia tilun ho talentu naturál ne'ebé konsege halo transkrisaun difisil balu. Ella, ha'u-nia oan feto ne'ebé sempre hatán ba pergunta hotu, no mós ajuda no suporta durante lemo-rai. Lillie, ha'u-nia oan feto, ba ninia suporta ne'ebé nunka falta. Ikus liu, ho laran tomak ha'u fó obrigada ba ha'u-nia kaben, Don Bennetts, ba ninia suporta husi A to'o Z.

ACKNOWLEDGEMENTS

I would like to thank all the Timorese musicians, artists, individuals and organisations whose contributions made this book possible.

First, the Timorese musicians who were so generous in sharing their performances and knowledge and who understood the need to make a permanent record of their musical culture. A special thanks to the first traditional Timorese musicians I met, Manuel Pereira and Pedro Tilman, who play *lakadou*. Their recording started the journey. Thanks to the directors of all the traditional music groups throughout East Timor who were so helpful and allowed access to their music.

The production of the book would not have been possible without the generosity and help of the United States Embassy in Dili, which through the U.S. Department of State granted a Federal Assistance Award. In particular Hans Klemm, who was the Ambassador at the time, and Embassy employees Jonathan Henick and Januario Soares. A special thank you to Tricia Johns, who sold my DVD set of Traditional Music to the American Ambassador Hans Klemm and initiated my introduction to him.

The Secretariat of State for Culture, specifically Virgilio Smith and Eugénio Sarmento, for sharing their knowledge. Lucas Serrao Lopes, for information about the Manta Ray Ceremony, and Nuno Olivera, who taught me so much. Karen Myers, who acted as the go-between for the many questions I had for people in the Secretariat of State for Culture.

I am most grateful to Richard Daschbach for his invaluable contribution on the music of Oekusi and to the Timorese from Oekusi, who entrusted him with the knowledge of their culture. Thanks to Atilio da Costa from Caritas in Oekusi, who also assisted with information on the music and Wade Freeman, who was vital as the go-between.

The artists at *Arte Moris* Art School and the founders Gabi and Luca Gansser, for their immeasurable generosity, hospitality, and assistance during the years of fieldwork. Thanks to all the artists who gave permission for their beautiful artworks to be published in the book. Particularly Tony Amaral, for his wonderful illustrations for the children's book, his artworks, his patience, diplomacy, humour and friendship on so many trips to Timor and for the long nights in Sydney translating recordings from Tetun to English. Pelle Pereira, for additional illustrations for the children's book. Cesario Soares Lourdes, for his images, untiring support, diplomacy and patience in the field. Alfeo Sanches Pereira, for his painting, good humour on journeys into the field and for his singing, Etson Caminha, Adilson Arintis da Costa Caminha and Ananias Carlos, for the Fataluku songs on the CD. Osme Gonçalves, for Fataluku songs, translations and stories and to Lely Barreto, for recording them.

The members of *Centro Audio-Visual Max Stahl Timor-Leste*, for assistance in many field trips. Particularly Max Stahl, for help, friendship and advice over the years of research. My warmest thanks also to his family who accommodated me on so many of my trips to Dili.

Thanks to Abel Guterres for his support and friendship over the years of research and to Gillian Howell, for information, advice and to her partner Tony Hicks for permission to use his photograph of the *kakalo*. Sejismundo Pedro Valentim Ray, researcher and photographer, whose help with transcriptions of songs and instruments of Ataúro, was much appreciated when time was running out.

Thanks also to Jose Trindade, for sharing invaluable knowledge of his culture with me and to Ameta Jorges Ximenes Mendonca, for information on the music and culture of the Makasae people. To Abilio dos Santos, for organising the demonstration of the *kakal'uta*. Iliwatu (Julianto Pereira), for information regarding the rarely seen *titir* drum.

For a memorable field trip, and chasing information needed at the end of the writing of the book, my thanks to Charline Bodin. Justino Valentim, for proof-reading all Fataluku texts and sharing the knowledge of instruments, songs and stories of Fataluku culture and for his generous hospitality. Melchior Dias Fernandes, for all the driving and roadside assistance in the last frantic trip before publication.

A special thanks to my editor and friend Susan Shineberg, for patience, scrupulous attention to detail, guidance and support throughout the writing of the book. To Vernon Tupper, Fiona Napier Flood, David Watson and Gail Clifford, who proof-read the English texts in the book. A huge thank you to Jonathan York and Milena da Silva for saving the day and for their wisdom, generosity and the Tetun version of the book. Kirsty Sword Gusmão, for proof-reading and offering advice with the children's book and to Ego Lemos, James Laidler, Wendy and Michael Dixon and Ingrid Bucens, for their advice regarding the children's book, my sincerest thanks.

Elizabeth Adams, for being hassled by me to check source material, names of people, instruments, songs and advice on the children's book. Marqi da Costa, for hospitality and allowing several invasions of his home during research trips. Marie Claire Sweeney, for friendship, good advice and support over the years we have known each other in Timor. Gail Clifford and Ceu Lopes Federer, for support, friendship and help through various stages of the project. Maire Sheehan, for being courier of illustrations from Timor to Australia. Anne Finch, for sound advice. Jenni Kanaley, for access to her tais collection, musical instruments, books, friendship and support.

Thanks to Louise Byrne, for sharing her knowledge and thesis and Patsy Thatcher for directing me to a valuable reading list. Ron Reeves, Ida Lawrence and Peter Dunbar-Hall for their help with the Indonesian notation system. Jim Chapman and Richard Vella, for their advice and guidance during the writing of the book.

I especially want to thank Rob and Martin Wesley-Smith, who initiated my first trip to Timor and for their continued friendship and support. To the designers of the book, Penelope and John Lee, I am in awe of their creativity, skills, professionalism and am indebted to their countless hours of meticulous work and advice with the design and layout of the book. A stunning result, thank you.

Warmest appreciation goes to my son Harry Bennetts, for proof-reading numerous texts and his great ears for some difficult musical transcriptions, to my daughter Ella, for her selfless assistance and support in field trips and beyond, and to my daughter Lillie, for her constant support, especially in the production of countless CDs and DVDs.

Finally, most heartfelt thanks go to my husband, Don Bennetts, for his enduring support and encouragement throughout it all.

Naran husi instrumentu múzika, knananuk no dansa sira diferente husi distritu ida ba distritu seluk, konforme ba lian inan ne'ebé uza. República Democrática de Timor-Leste rekoñese língua nasionál sanulu resin neen, no dialetu barak. Komu livru ne'e kona-ba múzika tradisionál Timor-Leste nian, Tetun ofisiál mak serve duni nu'udar lian tradusaun ba livru ne'e. Tetun mós hanesan lian komún iha fatin barak iha Timor laran. Livru ne'e sei publika tan iha lian Baikeno no Fataluku. Instrumentu lokál balu iha naran barak iha lian lokál sira. Porezemplu, *kakeit* bolu *knobe* iha Baikeno, *snarko* iha Mambae, *rai rai* iha Waima, *nagu* iha Makasae, *pepuru* iha Fataluku, no seluk tan. Iha mós diferensa kona-ba oinsá mak atu soletra ba instrumentu sira-nia naran. Dala ruma bele klarifika liu husi diskusaun ho povu sira iha foho ka iha Dili, maibé dala ruma la konsege klarifika. Nune'e ita haree variasaun uitoan iha ortografia ba terminolojia. Iha mós glossary, ka disionáriu ki'ik, ne'ebé bele ajuda atu klarifika liafuan hirak ne'e. Ha'u mós husu deskulpa ba ema sira ne'ebé koñese no hatene naran seluk husi instrumentu, múzika, ka dansa ne'ebé ha'u sei temi iha ne'e. Norma internasionál ida mak ita tenke uza letra boot ba letra primeira iha liafuan substantivu ne'ebé mak naran ba ema, fatin, ka dalen. Tanba ne'e, hakerek na'in ba livru ne'e deside atu halo tuir regra ne'e ba versaun Inglés no mós Tetun.

The names of musical instruments, songs and dances, vary from district to district depending on the mother tongue. There are sixteen national languages recognised by the Democratic Republic of East Timor and many dialects. As this is a book about the Traditional music of East Timor, it is appropriate that the indigenous, official language of East Timor, Tetun, be the language chosen for text translation, and it is also the lingua franca for much of the country. There are plans afoot for editions in Baikeno and Fataluku. Some of the musical instruments of East Timor are known by different names in several of the Timorese languages. For example, the *kakeit* (Tetun) is *knobe* (Baikeno), *snarko* (Mambae), *rai rai* (Waima), *nagu* (Makasae), *pepuru* (Fataluku) and so on. There were also discrepancies in the spelling of Tetun names for some instruments in several of the Tetun dictionaries consulted during the research and writing of the book. Consultation with Timorese in the districts where performances were recorded, and/or Dili, sometimes clarified a spelling, but at other times did not. Lautem is spelt Lautein to conform to the new codification of the Tetun language.

In the English texts an instrument will be referred to in italics by its Tetun (or other language) name with an English explanation, and for the rest of the article only by its Tetun name. A glossary is provided which may help to clarify an instrument name, dance or musical term. My apology to those who may recognise an instrument, song or dance by a different name or spelling. As it is an international convention to capitalise proper nouns, the author has decided to use that convention in both the English and the Tetun version.

INFORMASAUN KONA-BA MÚZIKA SIRA

Lee na'in no rona na'in sei nota karik katak transkrisaun husi múzika balu la hanesan ho ton ne'ebé ita rona iha CD. Ida ne'e tanba ha'u hakarak halo fasil atu aprende; porezemplu hakerek iha ne'e G maski F#. Ha'u mós uza sistema Indonézia nian, ne'ebé uza númeru, tanba Timoroan barak prefere ida ne'e duké sistema Osidentál nian.

LIA MENON HUSI TRADUTÓR SIRA

Livru ne'ebé ita boot kaer daudauk la'ós tradusaun diretu husi ninia testu orijinál ne'ebé hakerek iha lian Inglés. Livru ida ne'e bele bolu *versaun* husi ninia livru-inan. Iha buat balu ne'ebé autór hakerek ba lee na'in estranjeiru sira ne'ebé ema Timor hatene ona, no ami sente katak la presiza atu tradús buat sira ne'e.

Kona-ba ortografia, ami koko atu banati tuir sistema ne'ebé mak Institutu Nasionál Linguística (INL) publika tiha ona iha Disionáriu Nasionál ba Tetun Ofisiál, edisaun dahuluk, 2005. Ami fó agradese boot ba knaar na'in iha INL ne'ebé mak publika disionáriu ne'e. Iha liafuan balu mak ami uza iha livru ne'e ne'ebé seidauk hakerek iha disionáriu laran; se karik ami soletra sala, ami husu deskulpa.

Ami sente orgullu atu serbí povu Timor liu husi knaar ne'e. Ami espera katak livru ne'e bele fó inspirasaun foun ba Timoroan sira ne'ebé hakarak aprende kona-ba tradisaun sira ne'e. Importante liután, ami hanoin livru ne'e bele ajuda atu hametin identidade nasionál, habiit kultura, no promove respeitu-malu entre Timoroan sira.

Milena da Silva
Jonathan York

NOTE ABOUT THE SONGS

The musical transcriptions of some of the songs in the book does not match the pitch of the songs on the CD. For practical reasons it was thought best to put the musical notation in keys which are more accessible to those wanting to learn the songs: for example, G major rather than F# major. The Indonesian number system for music is also used, as many Timorese prefer this system for reading music rather than the Western notation system.

TRANSLATORS' NOTE

The translations from English in the book that you are holding are not direct translations but rather versions of its mother text. We felt that some of the things that the author wrote for non-Timorese readers did not require translation because they are common knowledge among the Timorese.

Regarding spelling, we've tried to follow the system of the National Linguistic Institute, as published in the National Dictionary of Official Tetun, first edition, 2005. We are very thankful for the work of the INL. We have also used some words that haven't made it into the dictionary yet; we apologise if we've guessed wrongly at their future official spellings.

We are proud to be of service to the Timorese people through this work. We hope this book will be a new inspiration for Timorese who want to study these traditions. More importantly, we hope this book will help to solidify the national identity, strengthen culture, and promote mutual respect among Timorese.

Milena da Silva
Jonathan York

MAPA DISTRITÁL BA INSTRUMENTU TRADISIONÁL SIRA

KAFU'I

• Found in most districts

TALA

• Found in all districts

KAKEIT

• Found in most districts

BABA DOOK

• Found in all districts except
  Oekusi and Ataúru

KARAU DIKUR

• Found the in the central
  mountain ranges

RAMA

TIHAK

BOBAKASA

BIJOL METO

KAKALO

KE'E

AU

KOKOTERE

ATAÚRU

O JAKO

DILI

BANO

LIKISÁ

BAUKAU

LAUTEIN

SENE

OEKUSI

AILEU

MANATUTO

ERMERA

VIKEKE

TITIR

BOBONARU

MANUFAHI

FIKU

AINARO

KOVALIMA

LAKADOU

KAFU'I OSSU

KAKAL'UTA

AILOOS

RARAUN

TITIR

TOHIN

xix

Lian Husi Klamar ne'e hamutuk ho ninia CD no DVD, fó ba lee na'in no rona na'in sira introdusaun ida kona-ba múzika tradisionál Timor-Leste nian, ho maneira ne'ebé informativu, dada atensaun, no nakonu ho imajen furak ba ita-nia matan. Até agora, múzika hanesan tradisaun ne'ebé orál, katak joven sira aprende husi katuas no ferik sira liu husi ibun ba ibun. Livru ida ne'e hanesan livru dahuluk kona-ba tópiku ida ne'e.

Múzika hola parte iha aspetu hotu iha moris Timoroan nian, no kanta hanesan instrumentu universál. Peskadór sira kanta bainhira hean sira-nia bero no soe rede ba tasi laran. Sira kanta ba lenuk no ikan lemur bainhira dada sira-nia rede. To'os na'in kanta ba karau sira no huu *kafu'i ka* flauta hodi bolu karau sira ne'e tama ba luhan laran. Dansa akompaña ho kanta bainhira ko'a hare. Ema gosta kanta bainhira halo knaar todan hanesan fai batar ka lere du'ut fuik husi natar laran, tanba kanta halo ita sente isin la baruk.

Múzika tradisionál iha papél importante iha serimónia relasiona ho moris to'os na'in nian, porezemplu kuda fini no ko'a hare.

Dansa mós hola parte importante iha múzika tradisionál Timor-Leste nian. Ema dansa durante serimónia hanesan harii *uma-lulik*. Dala ruma, ema dansa espontaneamente, porezemplu bainhira ko'a hare. Dansa prinsipál rua maka *dahur*, ne'ebé akompaña kanta, no *tebedai*, ne'ebé akompaña ho *baba dook* no *tala*. Iha serimónia nia laran, dala ruma *dahur* bele dansa kleur, bele kontinua nafatin ba oras barak nia laran.

Mitu sira no fiar ba lulik sasi hamutuk ho kultura muzikál tradisionál. Ida ne'e ita haree mós durante eventu sira iha sub-distritu, porezemplu, bainhira harii uma-lulik, bainhira bebé moris, ema mate, no festa kazamentu.

Instrumentu balu, hanesan *kakeit* no *lakadou*, iha mitu ne'ebé esplika oinsá instrumentu sira ne'e eziste.

Múzika nu'udar dalan ida ba istória orál nian husi knua ida-ida no hatutan dalas ba dalas husi jerasaun ida ba jerasaun seluk.

Maski moris iha kolonizasaun no okupasaun nia laran ba tempu barak, iha Portugál no Indonézia nia okos, povu Timor kria kultura ne'ebé riku no úniku, ho tradisaun muzikál di'ak tebetebes. Okupasaun ne'e hakanek tradisaun muzikál, liuliu durante tempu okupasaun Indonézia nian. Katuas ho ferik balu hato'o sira-nia laran rua namkait ho oinsá tradisaun muzikál sira ne'e bele moris ba nafatin iha futuru.

Ita bele nota katak múzika tradisionál iha distritu 13 nia laran dala ruma hanesan malu uitoan, maibé iha mós diferensa boot barak. Porezemplu, *pai koe-koe*, *kakalo*, no *titir* (ho forma hanesan ema mane nia isin) só bele hetan iha Lautein. *Rama* só eziste iha Ataúru. Tinan atus ida resin liubá, Ataúru iha *dadur* barak husi Portugál nia kolónia sira seluk, liuliu *São* Tomé no Prinsípe, no Angola. *Rama* ne'e kuaze hanesan ho instrumentu Angola nian ho naran ŋ!ao. *Bsoot* (dansa ida), *sene*, no *bano* la hetan iha fatin seluk, só iha Oekusi de'it.

Influénsia ba múzika tradisionál iha Timor-Leste mai husi dook, liu husi imigrante, negosiante, no esploradór sira, inklui mós husi Portugés no ema Indonézia sira. Timor mós hanesan dalan ba fatin komérsiu entre nusa Java no nusa Selebes. Ema Xina mai durante tinan atus ba atus nia laran hodi troka sasán, hanesan ho ema husi rai Arábia no Índia. Partikularmente influénsia Xina nian maka halo impaktu ba múzika, porezemplu *sit* sira husi Oekusi, no *nel* ne'ebé akompaña *bonet*, Oekusi nia dansa ida. Sinu besi ne'ebé kesi iha ain, ne'ebé uza iha *bsoot*, mós mai husi negosiante Xina sira. Ezemplu ida tan maka flauta *au* Likisá nian ne'ebé hanesan ho ida naran *pengbi* ne'ebé la barak ona no bele hetan iha rai Xina nia parte ida naran Guanxi Zhuang de'it. Fatin seluk ne'ebé mós kolónia Portugál nian hanesan Angola, Mosambike, no Malaka mós halo influénsia ba múzika Timor. Instrumentu sira hanesan *rama* no *kakal'uta* kuaze hanesan ho balu ne'ebé sei hetan iha rai Áfrika iha ema bushmen nia liman (tribu ida husi ema orijinál husi rai Áfrika). *Lakadou* no *kakalo* karik tama rai Timor ho ema Malaiu bainhira sira mai no halo migrasaun.

Illa Timor uluk fahe konforme reinu ne'ebé iha. *Wehali* maka boot iha parte Oeste. Reinu rua boot liu hotu maka naran Meto no Tetun sira (koñesidu ho naran Belu). Sira hela namkari iha Timor-Leste no Timor-Osidentál. Separasaun entre Timor-Leste no Timor-Osidentál ne'ebé kolonializmu kria la prevene múzika sira ne'e atu habelar bá mai iha fatin rua ne'e. Ezemplu di'ak ida mak *bidu tais mutin* akompaña ho *raraun* no kanta úniku. Ida ne'e sei apresenta nafatin iha Kovalima no mós iha Timor-Osidentál. Flauta simples ida naran *kafu'i* (ne'ebé uza kuak ida de'it ka la uza kuak) ne'ebé moris iha Bobonaru no Oekusi mós hanesan primu ida ba flauta ida naran *feku* ne'ebé ema uza iha Timor-Osidentál.

Ema Timor koñesidu ba ninia independénsia no fiar-an. Karik tan karakterístika sira ne'e mak ema Timor bele dezenvolve no la husik kultura múzika, maski influénsia barak tama hela de'it husi tasi sorin.

Ha'u hakfodak bainhira ha'u rona ema estranjeiru no ema Timor rasik dehan katak múzika Timor ladi'ak; katak repete hela de'it, no ita baruk atu rona. Ha'u la konkorda duni ho sira. Hanesan baibain, ita haree iha Timoroan sira-nia moris lororloron, fiar no kultura muzikál sira ne'e kompleksu no riku duni.

Margaret King kolia loos iha ninia livru *Eden to Paradise*, "Sira la hatudu buat hotu kona-ba sira-nia moris hodi buka oin."

Múzika tradisionál Timor-Leste nian hanesan parte fundamentál iha eransa kulturál, no mós hanesan buat ida ne'ebé halo ita sente orgullu nu'udar nasaun ida. Importante duni atu tau matan ba, no hatutan nafatin ba jerasaun sira tuir mai. Múzika sasi hamutuk ho aspetu hotu iha povu nia moris lororloron. Livru ida ne'e lori lee na'in halo viajen de deskoberatura ba múzika tradisionál, liu husi dansa, instrumentu sira, no istória, ho maneira ne'ebé kaer ita-nia atensaun.

Livru ida ne'e dokumenta istória muzikál ida ne'ebé to'o agora, so pasa husi ibun ba ibun.

Sounds of the Soul and its accompanying CD and DVD, introduces the reader to the traditional music of East Timor in a way which is engaging, informative, and visually rich. To date, this music has been passed on as an oral tradition and this is the first comprehensive publication on this subject.

Music is part of all aspects of Timorese life and singing is their universal instrument. Fishermen sing as they row out to cast their nets. They sing to the turtles and the dolphins when they bring the catch in. Farmers sing to the buffalos and play on their *kafu'i* (flute) to call them home. Songs accompany dances whilst husking the rice. Singing during mundane jobs such as pounding grain and weeding the rice paddies makes physical chores seem less monotonous. Traditional music also plays an important role in the special ceremonies for the various stages of the agricultural year, for example the planting and harvesting of crops.

Dance is an integral part of traditional music in East Timor. It's performed both on ceremonial occasions, such as celebrating the building of an *uma lulik* (sacred house), and spontaneously, for instance out in the fields when threshing the rice. The two main dances are the circle dance, *dahur*, danced to song, and the line dance, *tebedai*, danced to instrumental accompaniment of *baba dook* (drum) and *tala* (gongs). When danced during celebrations, the *dahur*, in particular, can go on for hours.

Myth and *lulik* (sacred beliefs - the spiritual root of life) are intrinsically entwined with the traditional music culture. This is particularly evident in the most important events in village communities, for example, the building of *uma luliks*, and in birth, death and marriage. The creation of certain musical instruments such as the *kakeit* (jaw harp) and the *lakadou* (tubed zither) are told through myths. Music is one of the ways the oral history of a village is passed on to successive generations.

Despite centuries of occupation, first under the Portuguese and then under the Indonesians, the East Timorese have developed a rich and unique culture, including an exceptional musical tradition. This musical tradition was so damaged or destroyed by the repression of the occupiers, particularly under Indonesian occupation, that there are concerns from elderly Timorese for its survival.

The allegiance of most Timorese is first to their clan and village and then to the nation. The many languages spoken in East Timor are from either Austronesian or Papuan sources. According to the linguist Geoffrey Hull, there are sixteen national languages recognised by the Democratic Republic of Timor-Leste. Twelve of these are Austronesian languages and four are of Papuan origin, which are the oldest languages in East Timor. There are many other languages and dialects in East Timor, demonstrating the eclectic nature of the origins of the East Timorese people. The physical differences of the Timorese from clan to clan is also evidence of these diverse origins, aptly summed up by the naturalist Henry Forbes who visited East Timor in the nineteenth century noting that, "...some Timorese had frizzy hair and some had straight hair, some tall, others again short and stumpy, while in others, characteristics varied so much that it is impossible to believe them to belong to a pure race." [1] These variations in origins may have contributed to the nuances in the culture, including the musical culture, from clan to clan.

Whilst some similarities in the traditional music can be found throughout East Timor, there are also distinct differences across the country's thirteen districts. For instance, the instruments used for scaring animals from the crops, the *pai koe-koe* (palm trumpet) and *kakalo* (bamboo slit drum), as well as the rarely seen *titir* (drum), shaped in the body of a man, are not found anywhere else in the country except in Lautein. The *rama* (mouth bow) is found only on the island of Ataúru. In the early part of the twentieth century Ataúru served as a penal colony for dissidents from Portuguese colonies, in particular the African colonies of São Tomé e Príncipe and Angola. The *rama* bears remarkable similarity to the ŋ!ao, a mouth bow played by the Bantu bushmen of Angola. The *bsoot* (a dance), the *sene* (gong ensemble) and *bano* (ankle bells) that accompany it, are not found in any other part of East Timor except Oekusi.

Influences on the traditional music of East Timor came from far and wide, by way of migration, traders and explorers, as well as via Portuguese and Indonesians. The island of Timor was on the trading network of East Java and Sulawesi, and there were centuries of trade with China, the Arab countries and India. In particular the trade with the Chinese has left traces on the traditional music, such as the *sits* (songs) and *nels* (chants) which accompany the *bonet,* one of the dances of Oekusi. The brass ankle bells which are worn for the *bsoot* are also thought to have originally come to East Timor with the Chinese traders. The remarkable similarity between the bamboo wind instrument the *au* from Likisá East Timor, and the endangered instrument the *pengbi* found only in Southwest China's Guanxi Zhuang region, attests to these influences. Countries colonised by the Portuguese, specifically in Africa (Angola and Mozambique) and South East Asia (Malacca), also influenced Timorese music. Instruments like the *lakadou* and *kakalo* (bamboo slit drum) may have found their way to East Timor with the Malay migrations.

Before Portuguese times, the island of Timor was made up of kingdoms. Wehali was the main kingdom to the West. The two largest ethno-linguistic groups were the Atoni (more commonly known as the Meto people) and the Tetun (Belu people) found in both East and West Timor. The separation of East and West Timor created by colonisation did not prevent the ebb and flow of musical influence between the two. Examples of this are the dance *Bidu tais mutin*, accompanied by the *raraun* (homemade guitar) and the unique style of singing that goes with it. This is performed in both Kovalima district, East Timor as well as in West Timor. The basic model of *kafu'i* (flute) with either no finger hole or just one, is found in the border districts of Bobonaru, Kovalima and Oekusi, East Timor. It is a cousin to the *feku* found in West Timor.

The Timorese are renowned for their independence and self-assurance. Perhaps it is these characteristics that have enabled them to develop and keep intact the traditional musical culture, despite various ethnic and multicultural intrusions.

Extraordinarily, some Westerners, and even some Timorese, have said to me that Timorese music is not good, that it is boring and repetitive. My observations defy such comments. Like so much of East Timorese life, the musical culture and associated beliefs are rich and complex, subtly and modestly conveyed. As Margaret King aptly observes, in *Eden to Paradise,* "They do not ostentatiously parade the realities of their way of life." [2]

East Timor's traditional music is a fundamental part of the cultural heritage and an integral part of its nationhood. It is vital that it be nurtured and passed on to successive generations. It is entwined in all facets of the life of its people. *Sounds of the Soul* takes the reader on a journey of discovery of the traditional music by way of dance, instruments, songs and stories in a presentation which is audiovisually engaging. The book puts on record a musical history which until now has only been passed on orally.

MÚZIKA TRADISIONÁL DANSA NIAN
TRADITIONAL MUSIC OF DANCE

Bainhira múzika iha, dala barak dansa mós iha. Ema hatudu dansa durante hala'o serimónia no ritual, porezemplu bainhira harii uma-lulik, ka selebrasaun bainhira tempu ko'a hare hotu. Dansa mós bele halo tanba ita hakarak dansa. Instrumentu no kanta sempre akompaña dansa ida.

Tipu prinsipál sira maka *dahur* (dansa iha liña kabuar), *tebedai*, no *bidu*, ne'ebé dansarinu sira forma liña. Dansa sira ne'e iha variasaun iha distritu hotu.

Dahur eziste iha fatin hotu iha Timor-Leste nia laran. Dansarinu sira-nia lian kanta maka múzika ba dansa ida ne'e. Dala ruma ema hatais roupa baibain, no dansa ne'e bele mosu derrepente de'it. Bainhira situasaun di'ak, *dahur* bele kontinua oras ba oras to'o madrugada.

Tebedai hanesan dansa liña ida ne'ebé akompaña ho *baba dook* no *tala* sira. Dansa ne'e serve duni atu simu bainaka, nune'e dansa ne'e iha ema mak fó treinu ba dansarina sira ne'ebé normalmente feto de'it. Dansarina sira hatais tais tradisionál. *Bidu* mós hanesan 'dansa liña' ida, ho *baba dook* no *tala* sira mak akompaña. Maibé, iha Kovalima, dansa hanesan *bidu tais mutin* sei akompaña ho *raraun* no mós kanta. *Bidu ailoos* akompaña ho instrumentu *ailoos*.

Liu tempu naruk, iha mudansa barak iha materiá ne'ebé dansarinu sira uza. Máskara husi ai, ne'ebé uluk avón sira uza iha dansa balu, ohin loron parese tara hela de'it iha didin iha uma-lulik sira, ka fa'an ba turista. Imajina to'ok dansarinu sira tau hela máskara; halo ema ta'uk karik. Hatais dala ruma la uza tais maibé uza fali au-tahan sira.

Dansa barak loos no oioin iha Timor-Leste nia laran, no balu konta istória, hanesan *makitit* no *maulelo*, husi Hatubuiliku. Dansa ne'e só dansa iha kalan, uza máskara, no konta istória kona-ba funu ida. Dansa sira ne'e kuaze la iha ona iha Timor-Leste. Uluk iha Oekusi iha dansa oin ualu; agora hela de'it haat. Ohin loron, iha festa kazamentu ka okaziaun ruma, joven sira hakarak dansa ho múzika Portugeza duké dansa tradisionál.

Where there is music there is often dance. Dance is performed for ceremonial and ritual occasions, such as during the building of the *uma lulik*, or to celebrate the rice harvest. Dancing can also just be for pleasure. Instruments or song accompanies dance.

The main forms of dance are *dahur*, a circle dance, and *tebedai* and *bidu*, which are line dances. The dances vary in each district of East Timor.

The circle dance, the *dahur*, is danced all over East Timor. The dancers sing to provide the music for the dance. People do not necessarily wear traditional dress for this dance and the dancing is often spontaneous. *Dahur*, if the occasion and atmosphere is right, will be danced for hours into the night.

The *tebedai* is a line dance accompanied by *baba dook* and *tala*. Regarded as a dance of welcome, it is often carefully choreographed, and mostly danced by women. Participants in the *tebedai* will wear traditional dress. The *bidu* is a line dance, which is mostly accompanied by *baba dook* and *tala*. However, in Kovalima district dances such as *bidu tais mutin* will be accompanied by *raraun* and singing, and *ailoos* accompanies the *bidu ailoos*.

The traditional dress for dance has changed over the years. Wooden masks, which today seem only to be used for adorning the walls of *uma luliks* or as items for tourists to buy, used to be worn for some dances. Masked dancers must have looked quite formidable. The dress was not always *tais*, but sometimes made from bamboo leaves.

Although there are many different dances in East Timor today, some of the more stylised ones tell a story: dances such as the *makikit* (eagle dance) or the *maulelo*, from Hatubuiliku, a dance theatre representing a war and performed only at night with masks. These dances have almost disappeared from East Timor. These days, young people in East Timor dance to Portuguese dance band music in preference to doing traditional dances for occasions such as weddings and parties.

above: Man from Mulo wearing tais mane with belak

top row: Dancers in traditional tais feto, kaebauk and morteen neck ornaments with raraun player, Joao Baros wearing a salenda and kaebauk

right: Grupu Rebenta dancer from Baukau, wearing tais feto and manu fulun headdress

far top right: Kaebuk with bird feathers
bottom right: Silver kaebauk with uma lulik motif

opposite page: Belak (left) and morteen (right)

Mane sira hatais *tais mane* no *salenda*. Sira kahe tais iha sira-nia hirus matan no tara *belak* iha sira-nia kakorok. Sira mós uza *keke* (kelu liman) ida ka rua iha sira-nia liman no dala ruma mós uza kelu ain ne'ebé halo husi *bibi nia fulun*. Iha sira-nia ulun sira uza *kaebauk* no tara *surik ho knuan*.

Feto sira hatais *tais feto*. Sira konde sira-nia fuuk ho ulusuku, uza sasuit osan-mutin. Dala ruma mós sira uza *kaebauk*. Iha distritu balu, hanesan Vikeke no Baukau, dansarinu sira (feto ka mane) uza *manu fulun* iha sira-nia ulun. Sira mós tara *morteen*.

The man wears a *tais mane* (man's cloth wrap) with a *salenda* (cloth sash) across his chest and a *belak* (medallion) around his neck; also a *keke* (ceremonial bracelet) or two on his arms and often an ankle adornment such as *bibi fulun* (goat hair). On his head he places a *kaebauk* (silver headdress) and he carries a *surik ho k'nuan* (sword and scabbard) to complete his outfit.

The woman wears a *tais feto* (girl's tube skirt). She draws her hair back in a bun to accentuate her beauty and decorates her hair with *sasuit sira* (silver hairpieces) or sometimes a small *kaebauk*. In some districts such as Baukau and Vikeke the dancers of both sexes will wear elaborate headdresses made of bird feathers, called *manu fulun*. Both men and women will often wear strings of *morteen* around their necks. These orange beaded necklaces are precious to the Timorese.

DANSA

Dahur

Dahur mak dansa iha forma sírkulu. Dansa ne'e eziste iha Timor laran tomak ne'e hanesan ritual ida hodi fahe buat ruma ba malu. Ema mós kanta hodi akompaña dansa ne'e. Dansarinu sira kaer liman, ka tula sira-nia liman iha dansarinu sira seluk nia kabaas. Ema ida sei hesi kanta ba dahuluk no ema sira seluk hatán iha koru nia laran. Sira kanta no dansa. Baibain mane sira dansa ho enerjia boot, tebe sira-nia ain, no feto sira dala ruma lakon balansu tanba dala ruma sira dansa ho movimentu neneik.

Dahur bele hatudu iha eventu oioin, hanesan atu simu ema, dansa iha serimónia nia laran, dansa hodi selebra progresu harii uma-lulik, hafoin ko'a hare, kazamentu, no eventu seluk tan. Dansa ne'e bele kontinua ba tempu naruk ho enerjia barak bainhira ema ba-rak mak partisipa, liuliu bainhira ema fahe tua sabu ka tua mutin ba malu. Hodi akompaña *dahur*, kada distritu iha sira-nia múzika rasik depende ba sira-nia lian inan. Melodia múzika ne'ebé sira uza karik pasa husi jerasaun ida ba jerasaun seluk, liafuan husi múzika sira ne'e dala ruma hanesan múzika kontemporánia. Ne'e hanesan reflesaun husi moris loroloron nian. Dala ruma liafuan sira ne'ebé sai hanesan piadas komika ba servisu governu nian, ka dala ruma mós kona-ba ema ida ne'ebé foin mate. Liafuan sira ne'e refleta parte oioin husi ema ne'ebé foin mate, kona-ba ninia istória mo-ris nian. Iha okaziaun hanesan ne'e *dahur* bele kontinua ba loron barak nia laran. Iha fatin seluk, liafuan sira ne'ebé ema kanta, sai hanesan istória komika, ka hanesan maneira ida ne'ebé joven sira uza hodi buka namorada ka namoradu.

EZEMPLU AUDIO *dahur*	**CD TRACK/FAIXA 19**
EZEMPLU AUDIOVIZUÁL	**DVD SENA 19-21**

Tebedai

Tebedai hanesan dansa tuir liña ne'ebé koñesidu tebes iha Timor. Iha kada distritu, kada aldeia, sira iha sira-nia estilu rasik hodi hatudu dansa ne'e. Bele uza dansa ne'e hodi simu bainaka ne'ebé mai vizita sira-nia fatin. Dansa mós uza hodi selebra buat ruma, simu sira-nia asua'in ne'ebé fila husi funu. *Tebedai* mós dala ruma hatudu iha serimónia tradisionál, hodi selebra progresu husi harii uma-lulik, no mós dala ruma hatudu iha festivál agrikultura nian, hanesan porezemplu ko'a hare, kuda hare, no seluk tan.

Ema uza *baba boot* no *tala* hodi akompaña *tebedai*. Ritmu ne'ebé prodús husi *baba dook* ne'e la hanesan husi distritu ida ba distritu seluk. Dansa sira ne'e tuir sira-nia koreografia ne'e furak no dansarinu sira hatais roupa tradisionál. Kada dansarina iha ninia *baba dook* rasik. Feto ida ka rua uza *tala*. *Tebedai* hahú ho feto ida dere *tala* ba dala 2 ka 3 hanesan sinál ida hodi hahú dansa ne'e. Dansarina sira seluk hatán ho baku sira-nia *baba dook*. Bainhira sira estabelese sira-nia ritmu, sira hahú sira-nia dansa. Dala ruma mós mane ida ka rua dansa hamutuk ho sira. Mane sira ne'e kaer sira-nia surik no dansa bá mai no halo lian halerik.

EZEMPLU AUDIO *tebedai* CD TRACK/FAIXA 14
EZEMPLU AUDIOVIZUÁL DVD SENA 13-18

Likurai

Likurai dansa ida ema Belu ninian, ne'ebé mai husi Timor-Leste no Timor-Osidentál. *Likurai* atu hanesan *tebedai*. *Bada dook* akompaña *likurai* ho ritmu lais. 'Liku' katak dansa ka halo isin parte leten nakdoko, liuliu liman sikun sira. Feto sira forma liña rua no dansa iha liña nia laran. Número ba feto sira ne'ebé dansa ne'e iha variasaun oioin maibé dala barak iha feto na'in 12 mak dansa. Ema mane ida de'it mak dansa iha feto sira-nia klaran.

Uluk, feto sira dansa *likurai* hodi simu asua'in sira bainhira fila mai husi funu. Asua'in sira lori sira-nia kroat ka espada, no dala ruma mós lori vitima nia ulun! Feto sira baku maka'as ho ritmu militár ida bainhira prosesaun ne'e la'o fali ba sira-nia knua. Tokadór didi'ak toka ritmu furak iha ritmu báziku (ne'ebé tokadór sira seluk toka) nia leten.

EZEMPLU AUDIO *likurai* CD TRACK/FAIXA 20
EZEMPLU AUDIOVIZUÁL DVD SENA 19-21

AI-KNANOIK LIKURAI NIAN

Ai-knanoik ida konta katak likurai hanesan samea ida mak dansa. Uluk, likurai ne'e iha feto 7 mak dansa, ne'ebé representa samea nia ulun 7. Mane ida ne'ebé dansa iha klaran representa fali katuas ida, ne'ebé tuir istória ne'ebá feto sira mak tau matan ba nia. To'o ikus feto sira ne'e fila an ba samea. Samea okupa fatin importante iha lisan no ritual Timor nian. Ohin loron bainhira halo dansa likurai, mane mak representa fali samea ne'e.

34

Bidu

Bidu hanesan dansa tradisionál tuir liña ne'ebé akompaña ho *baba dook* no *tala*. Dansarinu sira sempre hatais sira-nia roupa tradisionál. *Bidu* balu iha distritu Kovalima, porezemplu hanesan *bidu tais mutin* akompaña ho *raraun* no kanta mesak husi mane ida.

Dala ruma, ema uza *rabeka* atu kompleta parte ne'e. Kantór kanta ritmu ne'ebé livre no uza mós liña melodia tuir ritmu *sasando nian*. Sira-nia eskala mak C-E-F-G-B-C ka C-D-E-G-A-C.

Bidu ailoos mós mai husi Kovalima, no akompaña husi *ailoos*. Dansa ida ne'e no instrumentu ne'ebé akompaña, raru ona iha Kovalima. Fortunadamente, Sr. Johannes Bere husi Suai Loro ne'ebé agora dadaun serbisu iha Sekretária Estadu Kultura koñese no hatene dansa ne'e no nia mós hatene oinsá atu halo no halimar ho instrumentu *ailoos*. Sekretária Estadu Kultura iha Dili fó suporta ba Sr Johanes Bere atu hanorin dansa *bidu ailoos* ba dansarinu sira iha Suai Loro atu nune'e dansa ida ne'e sei la lakon.

Maski dansa ne'e populár duni iha tinan 1960, dansa ne'e prestíjiu uitoan no iha fatin barak la hetan koreografia ne'ebé hanesan.

| EZEMPLU AUDIO *bidu tais mutin* CD TRACK/FAIXA 9 |
| EZEMPLU AUDIOVIZUÁL DVD SENA 7-12 |

top left: The Likurai danced by young people from Kasa Bauk, where, these days the boy represents the snake.

bottom left: Likurai danced by young people from Leogore Maukatar.

top right: Dancers from Grupu Lafaek dancing the bidu tais mutin.

bottom right: Girls from Suai Loro play the ailoos for bidu ailoos dancers, wearing traditional tais feto, kaebauk and morteen neck ornaments.

Dahur

The *dahur* is a circle dance, danced throughout Timor, which is a ritual of sharing. Singing accompanies the *dahur*. The dancers hold hands, or place their arms over one another's shoulders while they sing. One singer will lead the song with a solo and everyone else joins in the chorus, dancing as they sing. Men tend to be more vigorous dancers, often lunging forward and slapping their feet on the ground. The women are sometimes caught off balance as they tend to dance in a more reserved manner.

Dahur can be performed for any occasions, such as a welcome dance, a ceremonial dance, to celebrate a stage in the building of an *uma lulik*, after the rice harvest, for a wedding or any other celebration. The more merry the company, the more energetic and prolonged the dancing, particularly when a few cups of *tua* (the local palm wine) is shared around, in which case the dancing might go on for hours. Each district has its own songs in the local languages to accompany the *dahur*. Whilst the melody of the songs may have been passed down through the generations, the words of the songs are often more contemporary, reflecting the everyday world around them.

The words might poke fun at the authorities, or may be about someone who has just died. The words reflect different parts of that person's life, telling their story. On such occasions the *dahur* may go on for days. In other *dahur* the words might tell jokes, or use flirtatious banter when young men and women are involved, as the *dahur* is the dance associated with the conquests of love.[3]

AUDIO EXAMPLE of the *dahur* CD TRACK 19
AUDIO VISUAL EXAMPLE DVD SCENES 19-21

Tebedai

Tebe means kick. *Tebedai* is a famous line dance well known in East Timor. Its literal meaning is 'following dance'. In every district each village has its own traditions for performing the *tebedai*. It can be a dance used to welcome visitors to a village. It is also the dance of celebration, or to welcome heroes home from war. *Tebedai* is often performed in ceremonies, work projects such as the different stages of building an *uma lulik*, or at the main agricultural festivals held through the year: the festival before planting, thanksgiving for the young corn, and the rice harvest.

Baba dook and *tala* accompany the *tebedai*. The rhythms provided by the *baba dook* vary from district to district. The *tebedai* is elaborately choreographed and the dancers wear traditional dress. Each dancer of the *tebedai* has their own *baba dook* to dance with. One or two women hold *tala*. The dance starts with one woman striking a couple of notes on a *tala* to signal the beginning of the dance, then the dancers begin to beat the rhythm for the dance on their *baba dook*. Once the rhythm is established they all begin to dance. Sometimes one or two men may join them, brandishing swords and even uttering cries.

AUDIO EXAMPLE of the *tebedai* CD TRACK 14
AUDIO VISUAL EXAMPLE DVD SCENES 13-18

Likurai

The *likurai*, is a dance of the Belu people, who are from East and West Timor. The *likurai*, is another form of the *tebedai*. It is a dance accompanied by the *baba dook* playing rapid rhythms. *Liku* means to dance or shake the upper body, specifically the elbows. The women form two lines and the dance is choreographed around these lines. The number of women can vary but quite often there will be 12 women dancing. One man will dance in the middle of the women.

In the past, women performed the *likurai* to welcome local heroes home from battle, who would be carrying their swords and at times, the heads of their victims! The women would beat a strong military rhythm as the procession made its way back to the village. The lead drummers played virtuosic rhythmic patterns over the steady rhythmic patterns of the other drummers.[4]

AUDIO EXAMPLE of the *likurai* CD TRACK 20
AUDIO VISUAL EXAMPLE DVD SCENES 19-21

LEGEND OF THE LIKURAI
Legend has it that the likurai is like a snake dancing. It used to be danced by seven women who represented the seven heads of a snake. The male danced in the middle of the women, representing the old man of history who was looked after by the women. The women would eventually turn into the snake. The snake has a special place in Timorese culture and rituals. These days when the likurai is danced, the man represents the snake.

Bidu

Bidu is a traditional line dance accompanied by instruments such as *baba dooks* and *tala*, and the dancers always wear traditional dress. Some *bidu* in the Kovalima district, such as the *bidu tais mutin* (a stately welcome dance), are accompanied by *raraun* and a solo male voice. On occasions, a *rabeka* (violin) may join the ensemble. The singer sings a free rhythmic pattern and the melodic line uses the pitches of the traditional *sasando* scale. The *sasando* is a tube zither from the Nusa Tenggara Timur province of Indonesia. The scales are either C-E-F-G-B-C or C-D-E-G-A-C.[5]

The singer may also use falsetto, yodel and other vocal effects, as well as long held notes interspersed with melismatic passages. The dancers synchronise with the rhythmic drone of the *raraun* and, holding their white cloth in front of them, perform a choreographed and elegant dance. They dress in *tais feto* and wear silver crowns and coin jewellery in their hair.

The *bidu ailoos*, also from Kovalima, is a dance accompanied by the *ailoos*. This dance and the instrument that accompanies it, the *ailoos*, have almost disappeared from Kovalima. Fortunately, Sñr Bere, who is from Suai Loro and is now working for the Secretariat of State for Culture, remembers how to dance *bidu ailoos* and make and play the *ailoos*. The Secretariat of State for Culture in Dili sponsored a project for Sñr Johanes Bere to teach the *bidu ailoos* to some of the dancers in Suai Loro so that it would not die out. Although popular in the 1960s, these days the *bidu* has little prestige and in many places is not even choreographed.

AUDIO EXAMPLE of the *bidu tais mutin* CD TRACK 9
AUDIO VISUAL EXAMPLE DVD SCENES 7-12

DANSA NE'EBÉ APREZENTA AI-KNANOIK

Makikit

Iha fiar ida katak Timoroan sira ne'ebé iha koneksaun besik ho rai bele iha komunikasaun ho manu sira ne'ebé lori mensajen, liuliu makikit. Tan ne'e, dansa ne'e orijinalmente konta istória makikit nian. Durante okupasaun Indonézia nian, dansa makikit sai hanesan símbolu ba kbiit no ukun rasik an, no ema Timor konsidera dansa ne'e hanesan mensajen husi ema ne'ebé sofre opresaun. Povu Suai respeita tebes ba dansa ne'e, no ema husi Suai mós halo dansa balu ne'ebé uza movimentu sira ne'ebé atu hanesan makikit nian.

Dansa *makikit* ne'e la'os de'it dansa ida ne'ebé fokus ba oinsá atu muda isin, maibé importante liu mak ninia drama. Dansa ida ne'e uza movimentu ne'ebé tuir forma jeometrika detallada tebes, no akompaña husi tambórista feto sira. Dansarinu sira hatais roupa tradisionál kompletu no mós uza ornamentu ulun nian ne'ebé kompostu husi manu fulun. Ohin loron *makikit* ne'e dansa hanesan *bidu* jeitosu no kontroladu ida, ne'ebé dansarina mak feto de'it. Múziku no antropólogu ida naran Margaret King hakerek deskrisaun di'ak loos ida kona-ba dansa makikit bainhira nia vizita Timor durante tinan 1960-1970:

"Dansa *makikit* ne'e konta istória ida kona-ba makikit inan sira ne'ebé halo hela sira-nia knuuk, hakru'uk hela hodi sara netik sira-nia fatin. Feto rua mak sai nu'udar makikit inan. Dansarinu mane na'in haat halimar hanesan makikit ne'ebé semo bá mai, buka hela balada ki'ik ruma atu han. Dala ruma feto sira book-an no muda tiha husi sira-nia pozisaun hakru'uk, ho liman rua dada naruk iha ulun leten, kaer hela selenda hodi fó impresaun hanesan liras ne'ebé halo arku bainhira sira semo sa'e hodi defende sira-nia knuuk. Depois, sira tun filafali ba pozisaun hakru'uk no mane 4 kontinua nafatin sira-nia movimentu hanesan kona-ba ataka no kontra-ataka. Durante ne'e *baba dook* lian la para até dansa remata."

Maulelo

Maulelo ne'e hanesan kombinasaun dansa, teatru, no serimónia ne'ebé úniku iha Hatubuiliku, maibé ohin loron ema ladún halo ona. Orijinalmente nia konta istória kona-ba funu entre liurai feto Builelo no liurai mane Maulelo. Serimónia ne'e só halo iha kalan de'it. Ema halo maskara husi ai, no oho bibi ida durante serimónia nia laran. Bibi hanesan símbolu ba funu nia vítima. Serimónia ne'e halo ba buat ida importante, hanesan bainhira presidente mai visita.

Iha tempu Portugés, Builelo no Maulelo sai hanesan figura sira ne'ebé representa di'ak no aat, hanesan símbolu ida ba Maromak no Diabu. Serimónia nia signifikadu relijiozu hahú iha ne'ebá.

EZEMPLU AUDIO *makikit* CD TRACK/FAIXA 21
EZEMPLU AUDIOVIZUÁL DVD SENA 19-21

Makikit

It was believed from times long ago that East Timorese most in touch with the land could communicate with the messenger birds, in particular makikit - the eagle, and thus this dance originally told the story of the eagle. During Indonesian occupation, makikit became the symbol of power and freedom, regarded as a messenger for the oppressed by the Timorese. Makikit is highly respected in Suai, and people from there perform dances which imitate its movements.[6]

The *makikit*, more a dance of mime and drama than of movement, is a stylised dance that uses intricate geometric patterns. It used to be accompanied on drums played by women. The dancers dressed in full traditional dress with elaborate headdresses made of feathers. These days it is danced as a *bidu* by female dancers, accompanied by *raraun* and *rabeka* and is more stylised and restrained in movement. Margaret King, musician and anthropologist, aptly described the eagle dance as she saw it when visiting Portuguese Timor in the 1960s: "The *makikit* tells the story of nesting female eagles, crouched protectively over their nests. Two female dancers portrayed the female eagles. The movements of attack and counterattack by the four male dancers

(eagles) suggested the movement of eagles hovering in search of prey. From time to time the women moved from their semi-crouched position, arms extended in graceful curves above their heads using scarves to add to the impression of arching wings as they rose to defend their nests. They returned to their crouching position and the four male dancers continued their mime of attack and counterattack, the *baba dooks* beating a relentless rhythm which continued until the dance ended."[7]

AUDIO EXAMPLE of the *makikit* CD TRACK 21
AUDIO-VISUAL EXAMPLE DVD SCENES 19-21

Maulelo

Maulelo is a combination of dance, theatre and ceremony unique to Hatubuiliku, but rarely performed these days. Originally it told the story of the war between Builelo, the Queen and Maulelo, the King, and is a ceremony only performed at night. Face masks are carved for the dance, and a goat is slain in the process of the dance as the symbol of the victim of the war. It is performed for special occasions such as the visit of a president. After the Portuguese arrived, Maulelo and Builelo became characters representing good and evil, that is, God and the Devil, and the ceremony's religious significance dates from that time.

INSTRUMENTU SIRA NE'EBÉ AKOMPAÑA DANSA

Baba

Baba mak tambór iha lian Tetun. Ninia arti seluk mak 'basa iha parte sorin ida de'it.' Iha *baba* oioin ne'ebé eziste iha Timor-Leste. Balu ema tara ka habit iha kabaas okos, balu ita harii tiha mak ita baku, no balu tau iha tara bandu nia sorin. Dala ruma mós ita bele hetan ema kesi ka tara *baba* sira ne'e iha lutu hun.

Iha mós *baba* ne'ebé uza ba *bidu* no iha fatin seluk, ema baku *baba* ba serimónia tradisionál no okaziaun espesiál. Tuir lisan iha kada distritu, ka kada knua, *baba* balu mane de'it mak bele uza, no *baba* balu feto de'it mak bele uza.

Kuaze *baba* hotu iha Timor halo husi ai no uza mós animál nia kulit hodi taka *baba* nia ulun. *Baba* balu asosiadu ho sermónia no ritual, porezemplu *tohin*. *Baba* tipu ulun ida barak mak eziste iha Timor-Leste, no iha mós *baba* tipu ulun rua, porezemplu *bobakasa* ne'ebé mai husi distritu Baukau.

Baba Dook

Tebedai mak dansa ne'ebé famoza liu iha Timor-Leste no Timor-Osidentál. Ema uza *baba dook* no *tala* hodi akompaña dansarinu sira. Só feto de'it mak bele baku *baba dook*, sira habit ka tara *baba dook* iha sira-nia kabaas nia okos.

Baba dook halo husi ai, no kulit ne'ebé taka *baba dook* nia ulun ne'e dala barak halo husi bibi nia kulit. Dala ruma mós ema uza niki nia liras ka parte liur husi karau nia rins. Lian ne'ebé prodús husi *baba dook* sira ne'e variadu depende ba kulit ne'ebé sira uza. Tamañu ne'ebé normal ba *baba dook* mak sentímetru 30 - 40 ho diámetru sentímetru 12-16.

Iha distritu, porezemplu Baukau, ita bele hetan *baba dook* ne'ebé bele halo vibrasaun. Ema uza tali tahan ka tali ne'ebé ema kesi haleu *baba dook* nia ulun hanesan ita bele haree iha imajen iha okos ne'e.

The drumhead of a snared baba dook, *showing the string drawn tightly across it, creating a buzz to the drum sound.*

EZEMPLU AUDIO *baba dook* no *tebedai* CD TRACK/FAIXA 14
EZEMPLU AUDIOVIZUÁL DVD SENA 13-18

Baba Dook Ki'ik

Baba dook ki'ik mak versaun ki'ik husi *baba dook*. Nia mós iha naran barak iha lian seluk, porezemplu iha lian Makasae ema bolu *titir*. Iha dimensaun oioin husi *baba dook ki'ik* sira ne'e. Son ne'ebé sira prodús ne'e moos liu no son sira ne'e dura ba tempu naruk uitoan.

Tala

Bainhira bainaka espesiál ida mai iha knua ida nia laran, ka fatin partikulár ida, ita sei rona ema dere *tala* hanesan símbolu ida hodi simu bainaka sira ne'e. Ita bele hetan *tala* iha rejiaun hotu iha Ázia Sudeste. Iha forma melódika no la melódika no dala barak mós ema uza ho instrumentu muzikál seluk.

Husi tipu sira ne'e hotu, *tala* ne'ebé ema barak koñese mak gamelan ne'ebé mai husi Indonézia. Iha mós tipu barak husi *tala* la melódika nian, no ita bele hetan barak iha Timor-Leste. Instrumentu ne'e mai ho naran oioin: iha lian Tetun ema bolu *tala*, iha lian Makasae ema hanaran *dadili*, iha lian Baikeno ema hanaran *sene*. Iha lian Mambae ema hanaran *dadil*.

Tala mak instrumentu ida husi instrumentu barak ne'ebé ema uza hodi akompaña tebedai. Jeralmente, feto ida mak dere *tala* no feto sira seluk iha *bidu tebedai* mak basa *baba dook*. Feto ida sei dere *tala* ba dala rua ka tolu atu fó sinál hodi hahú *bidu tebedai*.

EZEMPLU AUDIO *tala* CD TRACK / FAIXA 12
EZEMPLU AUDIOVIZUÁL DVD SENA 13-18

Ailoos

Ailoos mak ai-pedasuk silindru rua ne'ebé nia tipu lian hanesan xilofone. Baibain, iha feto nain 4 mak halimar. Feto ida-idak iha *ailoos* rua ne'ebé hatoba iha sira-nia ain. *Ailoos* sira ne'e nia tamañu maizumenus naruk sentímetru 50 no luan mak sentímetru 8 no afina ho ton oin ualu. Feto ida iha xave rua. Feto ida iha soprano nian rua, seluk iha alto nian rua, tuir mai iha tenor rua no ikus liu mak baixu rua. Feto sira ne'e tuur hasoru malu no baku *ailoos* sira ho ai-tanutuk ida ho tamanu sentímetru 20 x sentímetru 2. Tokadór sira mós bele tuur iha liña. Bainhira feto sira toka *ailoos*, dansarinu mane na'in rua ne'ebé hatais babuk, sei dansa tuir *bidu ailoos*.

EZEMPLU AUDIU *ailoos* CD TRACK/FAIXA 13
EZEMPLU AUDIU-VIZUÁL DVD SENA 13-18

Raraun

Iha mundu ida ne'e iha viola oioin, no iha rejiaun Ásia Sudeste no Áfrika, ita bele hetan tipu barak ne'ebé ema halo rasik iha uma. *Raraun* ne'e husi Timor-Leste. Nia la'os halo iha fábrika; nia halo iha uma de'it husi ai-pedasuk boot ida. Ninia tali haat, ne'ebé dada hakat ponte ida no metin iha prega ne'ebé hatama tiha iha kakorok nia kotuk. Afinasaun maizumenus hanesan ne'e: F#, G#, A#, C#. Bainhira akompaña *bidu tais mutin* ka *bidu makikit* (Kovalima nian) tokadór *raraun* sira toka la buti ho liman bainhira kanta.

Iha Timor-Osidentál iha dansa no instrumentu barak ne'ebé atu hanesan Timor-Leste nian, liuliu iha distritu sira iha fronteira, Kovalima no Oekusi. *Raraun* ne'e (naran *bijola* iha Timor-Osidentál) toka iha sorin rua hotu, faktu ida ne'ebé sujere katak instrumentu ne'e mai husi tempu koloniál. Iha fatin hotu *raraun* nia funsaun hanesan: atu akompaña *bidu*.

Influénsia husi Portugés sira kala hatudu an ho *raraun* ne'ebé atu hanesan ho cavaquinho, ne'ebé viola ho tali haat hotu, ne'ebé uza iha múzika xoro no samba.

EZEMPLU AUDIO *raraun* CD TRACK/FAIXA 9
EZEMPLU AUDIOVIZUÁL DVD SENA 7-12

46

Baba

Baba is the Tetun word for drum. It also means 'to play on one side'. There are many kinds of drums found in East Timor. Some are hand-held and others are freestanding. Drums are sometimes tied to a fence in order to play them. There are drums played for dances, while others can only be played during sacred ceremonies and on special occasions. Some drums can only be played by women and others only by men, according to the traditions of each village or district.

Most drums in East Timor are made of wood, with some kind of animal hide stretched across the drumhead. Drums like the *tohin* are associated closely with ceremony and ritual. The skin on the *tohin* is sometimes elaborately fastened to the drumhead with large wooden nails. Most of the drums in Timor are single-headed drums and conical in shape. There are a few double-headed drums, a fine example being the *bobakasa* from Baukau district.

Baba Dook

Below is one of the famous *tebedai* rhythms. It is played on the *baba dook*, a single-headed, hand-held drum, conical in shape and found throughout East and West Timor.

Tebedai is the most famous line dance in East and West Timor, and *baba dooks* and *tala* accompany the dancers. Only women play the *baba dook*, holding it under one arm and beating the drum skin with both hands.

Baba dooks are made of wood, and the skin stretched across the drumhead is mostly goat hide. Occasionally other skin is used, such as bat wing or the renal cortex from the kidney of a buffalo. The drum sound differs depending on what kind of animal skin is used.

Dimensions vary for the *baba dook*. The average size is 30 cm to 40 cm in length, with a diameter of 12 cm to 16 cm respectively.

In districts such as Baukau, you might see a snared *baba dook* being played. Snared *baba dook* have palm twine or string tied across the drumhead, as shown in the photo on page 43, and there is quite a buzz to the sound when the snared *baba dook* is hit.

AUDIO EXAMPLE *of baba dook* and *tebedai* **CD TRACK 14**
AUDIO VISUAL EXAMPLE **DVD SCENES 13-18**

Baba dook ki'ik

The *baba dook ki'ik* is a smaller version of the *baba dook*. It has other names in other languages, for example in Makasae it is called *titir*. Dimensions for the *baba dook ki'ik* vary, but are proportionally smaller than the *baba dook*, and the sound is brighter and less resonant.

Tala

When a special guest arrives at a village or other particular place, the sound of the gong will ring out to welcome them. Gongs are found throughout South East Asia. They can be either melodic or non-melodic, and are usually played in ensembles. Of these, the melodic gong ensemble of Indonesia, the gamelan, is probably the best known. There are also non-melodic gong ensembles, the variety mostly commonly found in East Timor. The Tetun name for gong is *tala*, although each language group in Timor has a different name for *tala*; for example, in Makasae, the name is *dadili*. In Baikeno, the language of Oekusi, it is called *sene*. In Mambae it is known as *dadil*.

In most of East Timor the *tala* are hand-held, which means the player holds the *tala* by a string handle and strikes it with a beater (see page 44). In East Timor, *tala* are mostly bossed, meaning that the centre of the *tala* is raised, while the rim can be shallow or deep. The *tala* in Baukau are bossed with a very deep rim like those found in central Java. The body of the *tala*, when struck, is the main resonator, vibrations of sound emanating from the centre. Often three or four pitches are possible on a bossed *tala*, with the pitches varying from instrument to instrument.

The *tala* is one of the instruments used to accompany the *tebedai*, a line dance famous in East Timor. Generally one woman plays the *tala*, while the rest of the women play the *baba dook*, a small handheld drum, dancing at the same time. One woman strikes the *tala* two or three times to signal that the dance may begin.

AUDIO EXAMPLE *of the tala* **CD TRACK 12**
AUDIO VISUAL EXAMPLE **DVD SCENES 13-18**

Ailoos

The *ailoos* is a wooden instrument that sounds a bit like a xylophone. There are normally four female musicians who each have two wooden keys lying across their legs. These keys are about 50 cm in length and 8 cm in width and are tuned to one of eight different pitches. One woman has two keys that are soprano, another two keys are alto, another two tenor and the fourth woman has two bass keys. The women sit in pairs opposite each other and play the keys by striking them with a wooden beater 20 cm x 2 cm. The players can also sit in a row. As the women play the *ailoos*, two male dancers wearing woven bamboo ankle bells, or rattles called *babuk*, dance the *bidu ailoos* to the music.

AUDIO EXAMPLE of the *bidu ailoos* CD TRACK 13
AUDIO VISUAL EXAMPLE DVD SCENES 13-18

Raraun

Lutes and guitars are found all over the world, and a number of homemade varieties can be found in Africa and South East Asia. The large homemade *raraun,* played in East Timor is initially carved out of a single piece of wood. It has four strings, stretched across a bridge and fastened onto pegs that plug into the back of the neckpiece. The approximate tuning of the strings are F#, G#, A# and C#. When accompanying elegantly choreographed line dances, such as *bidu tais mutin* from Suai Loro in the Kovalima district, the *raraun* player strums the same chord on the open strings whilst singing.

There are many dances and instruments in West Timor that bear similarity to those of East Timor, particularly in the border districts of Kovalima and Oekusi. The r*araun* (called *bijola* in West Timor) is played in East and West Timor, suggesting the instrument came from the times of Portuguese and Dutch colonisation.[8] In both countries the *raraun* is played for the same purpose to accompany *bidu* dances, the style of singing by the vocalist is similar too.

AUDIO EXAMPLE of the *raraun* CD TRACK 9
AUDIO VISUAL EXAMPLE DVD SCENES 7-12

Lakadou

Lakadou mak instrumentu tubu muzikál ida ne'ebé halo husi au ho medida oioin, maibé jeralmente maizumenus diámetru sentímetru 10 no naruk sentímetru 45.

Iha tempu uluk ne'ebá ema toka *lakadou* iha distritu barak iha Timor laran tomak, maibé iha tempu agora ema toka *lakadou* iha distritu ne'ebé uza lian Mambae: Ermera, Manufahi, Ainaru (liuliu iha Maubisi), inklui mós Likisá. Distritu sira ne'e hafatin iha foho ne'ebé malirin, nune'e au moris buras iha fatin sira ne'e no prodús au ne'ebé di'ak ba *lakadou*.

Toka *lakadou* hanesan tradisaun ida ne'ebé kontinua husi jerasaun ba jerasaun. Ema lubun balu de'it mak konsidera hanesan iha talentu ne'ebé natoon duni hodi toka *lakadou*; tanba ne'e buat ne'e hanesan buat karan ida ne'ebé sira-nia bei'ala sira fó.

Istorikamente, *lakadou* hanesan zither tubulár sira ne'ebé eziste tinan 2000 liubá iha fatin balu iha Ázia Sudeste. Zither tubulár hetan iha rai Malaiu (Lutong no Kecapi), hanesan prototipu husi zither tubulár barak ne'ebé hetan iha Ázia Sudeste, ne'ebé atu hanesan ho valiña husi Madagaskar. Instrumentu sira ne'e hotu nia forma hanesan ho *lakadou* duni.

Iha laloran migrasaun tolu ne'ebé tama Timor-Leste. *Lakadou* bele karik introdús husi migrasaun datoluk nian; proto-Malaiu sira husi Xina do Súl no Indoxina Norte. Lia Na'in sira fiar katak *lakadou* eziste ona iha Timor molok ema Portugál sira tama Timor-Leste.

Iha variasaun oioin ba númeru tali iha *lakadou*. Normalmente entre tali 6-18 mak ko'a tiha husi au nia kulit. Tali ida-idak suporta ho ponte ki'ik ida ne'ebé bele muda hodi afina tali sira ne'e.

Afinasaun *lakadou* bazeia ba ton ne'ebé knananuk ne'ebé atu hananu presiza. Tali ida nia ton bele tau iha ne'ebé de'it, konforme númeru tali ba kada instrumentu. Afina tiha ona, tali ida kaer ninia nota kleur. Neineik, tali sira estika an no lakon afinisaun, no presiza afina filafali.

Espasu entre tali sira ne'e mak sentímetru1 ka 2. Se karik tali ida kotu, bele halo tan ida iha fatin mamuk entre tali sira. Bainhira tali reserva aat ona, *lakadou* ne'e labele uza ona no tenke halo *lakadou* foun ida. Iha tubu nia rohan ida-idak iha buat ida hanesan sintu ne'ebé sasi tiha husi tali tahan ka husi au.

Iha *lakadou* nia kotuk, ema bahat kuak ida ho tamañu sentímetru 3 x 8 ne'ebé ajuda hodi halo lian boot ka maka'as. *Lakadou* nia rohan ida nakloke, ida fali taka husi au nia selat naturál, ho kuak ki'ik iha klaran. Tokadór uza ninia liman fuan ida hodi taka ka loke kuak ne'e hodi muda nia ton, bainhira nia dere hela tali sira ho ai-mihis ka plektru (pick) ne'ebé halo husi *karau dikur* ka au. Plektru ne'e mós uza hodi kose hamos fatin entre tali sira, nune'e ninia lian sai boot no moos liután.

Lakadou ida bele uza durante tinan 5 ka 6 nia laran; menus kuandu mirain han tiha.

Ema ida ka rua, mane ka feto bele toka *lakadou*. Se na'in rua karik, presiza ema rua ne'e iha koneksaun espesiál, atu bele sente espíritu sira bainhira sira toka. Bainhira na'in rua mak toka, ida dere tali sira no kaer *lakadou* rabat nia isin, ho kuak iha kotuk hodi haboot ninia son. Múziku ida fali uza ai-mihis rua (ninia tamañu varia husi sentímetru 1/4 x 24 ate sentímetru 1/2 x 38) hodi dere tali sira besik rohan ida, nune'e kria son ho kualidade barak.

Bainhira ema ida de'it mak toka, nia bele hamriik no kaer *lakadou* hanesan viola ki'ik no dere ho plektru ida, ka nia bele tuur no hatoba *lakadou* iha ninia kelen leten, no dere nia ho ai-mihis sira. Dala barak ita uza hodi akompaña hananudór no bidudór sira. Kuandu ema kanta hamutuk ho *lakadou*, lian *lakadou* nian mak importante liu duké hananudór nian.

| EZEMPLU AUDIO *lakadou* | CD TRACK/FAIXA 1 |
| EZEMPLU AUDIOVIZUÁL | DVD SENA 1-6 |

ISTÓRIA LULIK Kona-ba kriasaun *lakadou*, ne'ebé konta husi Matebian Floréncia da Costa, tokadór ida husi Holarua, sub-distritu Same.

Ulukliu, bainhira Timor-Leste sei joven, iha maun alin na'in rua. Iha loron ida, sira la'o halimar iha ai-laran fuik no bainhira rai-nakaras, sira realiza katak sira fahe malu tiha no la hetan malu. Alin ta'uk, tan ne'e nia fila-an sai tiha au-hun ida, ne'e para balada fuik sira labele hakanek nia. Maibé nia la konsege fila-an ba nia an rasik. Ninia maun ba buka nia. Ikus mai, maun rona anin ida ne'ebé lori ninia alin nia 'lian kanta' mai ninia tilun. Nune'e maun hetan au-hun ne'ebé nia alin fila an ba. Espíritu sira mai no hatete ba maun atu tesi tiha au nia parte leten, no hanorin nia oinsá atu halo lakadou. Nia komesa toka, no nia sente katak nia hetan fali ninia alin mane.

Lakadou

The *lakadou* is a tube zither made of bamboo and varies in size, the average being about 10 cm in diameter and 45 cm in length.

In the past the *lakadou* was played in most of the districts of East Timor, but today it is mostly played in the Mambae-speaking districts: Manufahi, Emera, Ainaro and Maubisi, as well as Likisá. These districts are located in the cooler mountain regions, which is where the best bamboo for making the *lakadou* grows. Generally the top segment of the plant is used.

The playing of the *lakadou* is passed on as an oral tradition to each generation. Only a few people are considered talented enough to be able to make the *lakadou*, which is a gift said to be passed on by the ancestors.

Historically, the *lakadou* is related to the tube zithers found over 2000 years ago in parts of South East Asia. The tube zithers found in Malaysia (Lutong and Kecapi) were prototypes of many of the tubes zithers found in South East Asia, which in turn created the *valiha* from Madagascar. All look very similar to the *lakadou*.

There were three waves of migration to East Timor, and the *lakadou* quite possibly arrived with the third migration, the proto-Malays from South China and North Indochina. The *Lia Na'in* (keepers of the word) who live in a number of districts, believe the *lakadou* dates back in East Timor to pre-Portuguese times.

The number of strings on the *lakadou* varies. Usually between six and 18 strings are cut from the surface of the bamboo. Moveable bamboo bridges are placed under each string, and the strings are tuned by sliding the bridges along underneath them.

Tuning of the *lakadou* is based on the pitch of the song that is about to be sung. The pitch of the strings is arbitrary, depending on the number of strings for each instrument (major 2nd to a perfect 4th). Once tuned, the pitch stays in place for a long time. Eventually the bamboo strings stretch, and need to be re-tuned.

The gap between each string is 1 or 2 cm, so that if a string breaks then another can be cut in the gap between to replace it. When the back-up string breaks, the *lakadou* cannot be used any more and a new instrument must be made. At each end of the tube where the strings begin there is a plaited band of palm-string or bamboo.

On the back of the *lakadou* is a carved-out hole (3 cm x 8 cm) that helps amplify the sound. One end of the tube of the *lakadou* is open, the other closed by the natural nodes of the bamboo, with a small hole in its centre. The player uses the index finger to cover and uncover this hole, thus varying the tone, whilst strumming the instrument with a plectrum made from buffalo horn or bamboo. The plectrum is also used to clean the grooves between the strings, which helps sound production. Each *lakadou* lasts up to five or six years, unless termites eat them.

The *lakadou* can be played solo, or by two musicians, male or female. If there are two players they must have a special connection, so they can sense the spirits when they play. When there are two musicians, one musician strums the strings and holds the *lakadou* against their body with the hole at the back, to amplify the sound. The second musician uses bamboo beaters (1/4 cm x 24 cm to 1/2 cm x 38 cm in size) to strike the strings at one end, thereby creating several layers of sound. When there is one player, the *lakadou* is either held across the body and strummed with a plectrum, or the player sits on the ground with the *lakadou* balanced along their legs and plays by striking the strings with the beaters.

The *lakadou* is often used to accompany singers and dancers. When songs are sung with the *lakadou,* the sound of the *lakadou* is more important than the song.

AUDIO EXAMPLE of the *lakadou* CD TRACK 1
AUDIO VISUAL EXAMPLE DVD SCENES 1-6

A LULIK STORY ABOUT THE CREATION OF THE LAKADOU
as told by the late Florencia da Costa, a *lakadou* player from Holarua, a sub-district of Same.

A long time ago when East Timor was a very young country, there lived two brothers. One day they wandered into the forest and soon became separated as night began to fall. The younger brother then became very frightened and so he turned himself into a bamboo plant in order that no wild animal would hurt him, but he couldn't turn himself back into a man again.

When he didn't return home, the older brother came looking for him. Eventually he heard him singing in the wind and found the bamboo plant that was his brother. The spirits came to him, told him to cut the top segment off the bamboo and taught him how to make the lakadou He started to play it, and felt as if he had found his younger brother.

53

54

MÚZIKA TRADISIONÁL OEKUSI NIAN
TRADITIONAL MUSIC OF OEKUSI

Introduction
INTRODUSAUN

Richard Daschbach SVD kontribui kapítulu ida ne'e padre ida husi rain EUA, ne'ebé hela no serbisu iha Timor-Leste hahú kedas husi tinan 1966. Ninia hakarak atu ajuda povu Timor, metin nafatin to'o agora. Padre ne'e estabelese uma ida ba labarik kiak sira ho naran Topu Honis iha Oekusi. Topu Honis signifika katak 'Matadalan ba Moris' no kontinua ajuda labarik sira husi tinan 3 to'o tinan 18, fó fatin seguru ne'ebé nakonu ho domin no edukasaun. Padre Richard hetan respeitu barak husi povu Oekusi. Aleinde ninia atensaun ba povu nia presiza espirituál no fó mahon ba labarik oan-kiak sira, nia ho aten barani proteje ema barak durante destruisaun ne'ebé akontese hafoin referendum ba ukun rasik an iha tinan 1999.

Oekusi is an enclave in the middle of the north coast of West Timor and is isolated from the rest of East Timor. The main route between the two is a long ferry trip of more than ten hours. Perhaps due to this remoteness the traditional music of Oekusi is distinctive and quite different from the rest of East Timor. The traditional music of Oekusi bears similarity to the traditional music of West Timor. Many of the people of West Timor and Oekusi are from the same ethno-linguistic group, the Atoni people, more commonly known as Meto. The dances of Oekusi have no equivalent in the rest of East Timor. The music, dance and song of Oekusi are a fragile culture and half the original dances have vanished. The centuries of colonisation and conflict between the Dutch and Portuguese and in more recent times the Indonesians, have perhaps all contributed to the demise of the traditional musical culture. Another factor could be that much of the language of poetry, prose, chants and songs is classical Metonese, a language which is not generally spoken or understood today.

This chapter is contributed by Richard Daschbach SVD, a US priest who has lived and worked among the Timorese people for 45 years. He first came to Timor in 1966 and has remained steadfast in his desire to help children and families in this needy nation. He established a children's home Topu Honis in Oekusi, meaning "guide to life" which continues to serve many children ranging in age from three to 18 years as a refuge of love and nurturance. He is well respected by the populace of Oekusi. Besides attending to their spiritual needs and sheltering orphans and neglected children, he courageously helped protect many during the destruction following the vote for independence in 1999.

Orijinalmente iha dansa ualu iha Oekusi, mak :

1 Bilut
2 Takanab
3 Bsoot and Lelan
4 Bonet
5 Muiskatele
6 Oebani
7 Fekula
8 Kure

Husi dansa sira ne'e, balu lakon ona. Ohin loron, só dansa oin haat mak ema sei halo regularmente: *bilut, takanab, bsoot,* no *bonet. Bilut* ne'e dansa ida ne'ebé ema sei dansa mesak, inventa hela ninia jeitu úniku.

Takanab

Takanab ne'e poezia ne'ebé sani husi maksani ida no koru ida. Sira uza dalen klasikál Metonese nian. Dala ruma ema uza *takanab* hodi simu bainaka espesiál ne'ebé mai vizita. *Takanab* mós hatudu iha serimónia tradisionál, porezemplu hanesan molok no depois harii uma-lulik, uza hodi fó agradese ba natureza bainhira ema ko'a hare, bainhira mane ida hakarak husu feto ida atu kaben ho nia. *Takanab* sempre kona-ba tópiku ruma, ne'ebé aumenta ho fraze balu ne'ebé sempre uza iha *takanab*. *Takanab* bele mós sai nu'udar bemvindu bainhira atu hatudu dansa tradisionál Oekusi nian.

Takanab ne'e arte, ne'e duni maksani tenke hatene didiak oinsá mak halo. Normalmente lia-na'in mak sei sani *takanab* hanesan poezia, ho liafuan no fraze ne'ebé repete tuir ritmu. Koru hatán ho parte segundu. Ritmu la'o nafatin ho pulsu (raan-tukun) ne'ebé metin duni.

Ezemplu *takanab*:

Maksani: hit 'tol ama tniku neno I nbi kuan Kutet ma...
Koru: bale Kutet

Maksani: ka neu fa sa, neuba he tsimo hit Anaet; tsimbe ma...
Koru: tataim'e
Maksani: neno I fef menu namnekben, fef kiti ma...
Koru: neki nao
Maksani: nek mese ansao mese; fef keti kuk ma...
Koru: han keti

Liafuan "ma" (no) dada naruk tiha, hanesan sinál ida ba koru atu responde. Koru tama ho sinónimu sira ne'ebé nato'on.

Tradusaun:

Maksani: ita halibur malu iha ne'e ohin iha knua Kutet no...
Koru: fatin Kutet nian
Maksani: la iha razaun seluk; ita atu simu ita-nia respeitadu
Koru: ...simu nia
Maksani: Ohin ibun moruk la iha tiha ona, ibun moruk no
Koru: ...la iha tiha ona
Maksani: Mota sulin lori tiha ona sira, anin huu maka'as
Koru: ...lori tiha sira
Maksani: Agora ita fuan ida de'it, susun ida de'it, ita-nia ibun kolia loos
Koru: ita-nia ibun kolia loos

Bainhira halo *takanab*, liafuan no fraze barak mak iha liu tiha sinónimu ida. Korista balu bele hatán ho ida, no seluk hatán ho liafuan seluk. Dala ruma maksani haluhan atu dehan "*ma*," ka kolia ladún moos, ka koru la hanoin lais atu bele hetan sinónimu ne'ebé adekuadu. Iha kazu sira ne'e maksani mak fó, no kontinua de'it. Dala ruma mós koru tama derrepente de'it ho sinónimu ne'ebé ema la espera. Dala ruma maksani nia lian la boot ida, ka nia moedór, ka nia hemu tiha tua atu sai barani maibé nia bilan fali. Resultadu husi buat sira ne'e hotu bele halo *takanab* kapás ida, maski la perfeitu. Maksani ho lian boot, ne'ebé hanoin hetan liafuan *takanab* nian, sente konfortavel bainhira kolia iha públiku, no treinu tiha ona hamutuk ho ninia koru, bele kria *takanab* di'ak tebes.

Koru ne'e baibain kompostu husi katuas sira de'it, tanba mane sira ne'ebé seidauk idade boot kala la hatene sinónimu sira ka

fraze sira hotu ne'ebé *takanab* uza, nune'e sira ladún komprende karik ka ladún interese. Linguajen klasikál la'os buat ida ne'ebé interesante ba ema hotu.

Verbu sira iha lian Meto nian la indika futuru ka pasadu; tempu ita komprende liu husi hanoin ne'ebé iha. (Futuru no pasadu bele hatudu sai ho liafuan seluk, la'ós verbu ida). Ema Meto sira-nia moris loroloron tradisionál liu no ketak husi grupu seluk. Meto sira moris iha presente nia laran, agora, maibé pasadu (istória, ai-knanoik, mitos, bei'ala sira no buat ne'ebé bandu) mós importante ba moris knua nian. Iha kultura meto nia hanoin, futuru no pasadu homan hamutuk; ida ne'e susar ba ema estranjeiru atu komprende karik.

EZEMPLU AUDIOVIZUÁL *takanab* DVD SENA 7-12

Originally there were eight dances in Oekusi :

1 Bilut
2 Takanab
3 Bsoot and Lelan
4 Bonet
5 Muiskatele
6 Oebani
7 Fekula
8 Kure

Half of these dances have vanished. Today, only four are regularly performed: the *bilut*, *takanab*, *bsoot*, and *bonet*. The *bilut* is a dance which people dance by themselves creating their own personal style.

Takanab

The *takanab* is a poetic recital chanted by the reciter and a chorus, using mainly classical Metonese language. On arriving for a special visit, respected guests may be greeted with a recitation of the *takanab*.

It is also performed in traditional ceremonies, such as before and after the building of a traditional house, to give thanks after the harvesting of the crops or when a man seeks a woman's hand in marriage. The subject matter is topical, with stock phrases being added to it. It can also be the welcome that precedes performances of traditional dances of Oekusi.

The *takanab* is an art form, so the reciter must be someone who can actually do it. Usually the *ketua adat* (head of the traditional house) will recite it as poetry - words and phrases using alliteration, rhythm and doublets. The chorus answers the second part of the doublet. The rhythm of the chant maintains a steady pulse.

An example of a *takanab*:

Reciter: hit 'tol ama tniku neno i nbi kuan Kutet ma...
Chorus: bale Kutet

Reciter: ka neu fa sa, neuba he tsimo hit Anaet; tsimbe ma...
Chorus: tataim'e
Reciter: neno i fef menu namnekben, fef kiti ma...
Chorus: namnekben
Reciter: noel nsai neki nao, ain nfu ma...
Chorus: neki nao
Reciter: nek mese ansao mese; fef keti kuk ma...
Chorus: han keti

The word "ma..." (and...) is drawn out, as a sign for the chorus to respond. The chorus comes in with appropriate synonyms.

Translation:

Reciter: We've gathered and gathered (here) today in the village of Kutet and ....
Chorus: ... the place of Kutet
Reciter: For no other reason than to receive (welcome) our distinguished visitor; receive him and ...
Chorus: ...receive him
Reciter: Today bitter mouth has disappeared, sour mouth and ...
Chorus: ...has disappeared
Reciter: The river has flowed and taken (them) away, the wind has blown and ...
Chorus: ...taken (them) away
Reciter: (We are now) one heart and one breast, our mouths well ordered, and...
Chorus: ...our voices well ordered

In the execution of a *takanab*, many words and phrases have more than one synonym. Some in the chorus may answer with one, while others answer with another. Sometimes the reciter will forget the "*ma*", or won't enunciate it clearly, or the chorus won't think quickly enough for an appropriate synonym. In those cases the reciter will just supply it and go on. At times the chorus will come in on its own with an unexpected synonym. Occasionally the reciter has a voice that doesn't carry, or is self-conscious and unnerved, or has drunk a bit of alcoholic *tua* to steel himself but only wound up getting befuddled. The result of all of this can still be a good *takanab*, but not an optimal one. The reciter with a clear

voice who knows his *takanab* language, is at home speaking in public and who has practised ahead of time with his chorus, will create a *takanab* of classical elegance.

The chorus is traditionally composed of older men, as the young men may not know many of the synonyms or figures of speech that lace *takanabs*, and so find their understanding limited and they are probably not so interested anyhow. Classical language, like classical music and drama in our culture, is not for everyone.

The Metonese verb is tenseless, tense being expressed by the thought, rather than the verb ensconced in the thought. When future or past is expressed, or implied in the thought, it would be redundant for a verb to also express it. Past and present are also expressed by auxiliary words, not by verbs.

The Metonese have an insular and traditional way of life that exists pre-eminently in the present. However, the past (history, lore, ancestors and taboos) is very much a part of Metonese village life. In Metonese thought, past and present are interwoven in a way that the Western mind might find difficult to comprehend at first.

AUDIO VISUAL EXAMPLE of the *takanab* DVD SCENE 7-12

Bsoot No Lelan

Biar termu jerál ba dansa ho sinu-ain mak *bsoot*, teknikamente liafuan '*bsoot*' ne'e refere de'it ba pasu sira ne'ebé ema mane uza. Mane sira dansa *bsoot* hanesan ne'e: hiit ain ida no sama rai maka'as fali, muda ain ida fali mai kotuk, no presiza ain rua muda la para. Maski nune'e, dansarinu bsoot ida ne'ebé ba Jakarta (ho dansarinu didiak sira seluk hodi fó esposisaun kona-ba dansa ne'ebé uza sinu-ain) kuaze la hiit ain liu, no nia halo hela *bsoot*, la'ós *lelan* ne'ebé versaun *bsoot* feto nian. Pasu feto sira nian iha variasaun menus entre ema ida-idak kuandu kompara ho mane nian. Normalmente dansarinu sira husi *bsoot* no *lelan* kesi *bano*, maibé dansa sira ne'e la presiza halo ho *bano*. Bele halo ho manu fulun kesi ba ain, bibi nia hasan-rahun, ka tali tahan homan hodi forma kubu sira, ho ai-pedasuk ki'ik iha kubu ida-idak nia laran, ne'ebé halo lian ki'ik bainhira ema dansa.

Ohin loron *bsoot* hanesan forma dansa livre, ho dansarinu ida-idak kria rasik ninia jeitu individuál. Uluk, dansa ne'e formál, no mós iha *bsoot* oioin. Buat tara husi ain tipu seluk, no mós tipu *bsoot* seluk, la iha tiha ona. Iha lia-anin ka rumores balu ne'ebé dehan katak iha fatin isoladu ruma sei iha ema ne'ebé hatene oinsá atu dansa *bsoot* oin seluk, no dala ruma mós halo. *Bsoot* ne'e serve ba buat barak, liuliu selebrasaun hanesan kazemantu.

Iha tinan 1981 padre Richard Daschbach haree *bsoot* formál ida iha Oekusi nia knua ida ne'ebé sei mantein sira nian kultura tradisionál maibé dezde tempu ne'ebá to'o agora nunka haree fali. Sasán tara iha ain ne'ebé tipu seluk, no *bsoot* tipu seluk atu rai de'it ona iha arkivu nia laran, hein ema kuriozu ruma ka estudante ne'ebé buka hatene kona-ba lisan uluk nian.

Durante *bsoot*, feto sira dere *sene* no *ke'e*. Dansarinu sira dansa tuir *sene* la'os *ke'e*. *Ke'e* nia lian *boot*, ho ton ida ne'ebé nakonu, mak halo múzika ne'e sente forsa liu tan. Dansarinu sira no tokadór sira bele ipnotiza husi lian *ke'e* no *sene*.

Bainaka estrangeiru ida konta istória kómika ida: *ke'e* no *sene* halo lian runguranga, tuir ninia hanoin. Dansarinu sira la'o bá-mai, la hakat hamutuk ida. Sira para no haruka tokadór *sene* sira

atu halot sira-nia ritmu, tanba sira toka sala. Feto sira troka fatin, no hahú filafali. Bainaka hanoin katak múzika agora aat liután, maibé dansarinu sira agora hakat hamutuk hanesan ema ida de'it. *Sene* sira di'ak loos ona, maibé bainaka nia tilun mak la komprende ida ne'e.

Kona-ba *bano* (ne'ebé tuir matenek na'in nia hanoin, *bano* ne'e mai husi Xina), ne'ebé hanesan ornamentu-ain Timor nian, bele haree ba posibilidade rua:

Dahuluk: Timor nia ornamentu-ain iha ona, antes *bano* tama husi Xina. Maibé *bano* populár kedas tanba dansarinu sira gosta kesi *bano* iha sira-nia ain.

Daruak: *Bano* mai uluk, maibé komu sira karun no susar atu hetan, ema sira ne'ebé labele sosa uza fali instrumentu-ain seluk.

Bano

Antropólogu kulturál ida ba vizita Oekusi no haree dansa ruma ne'ebé uza *bano*. Nia husu tuir maibé ema hotu la hatene *bano* nia fatin orijinál mak iha ne'ebé loos. Nia kuriosu, maibé labele aprende buat ida. Depois, bainhira nia bá lemo-rai iha Xina nia parte norte, nia tama muzeu ida no iha ne'ebá nia haree *bano* ne'ebé hanesan duni ho Timor nian. Xefe muzeu dehan katak, 'Uluk tinan rihun ba rihun liubá, ami-nia bei'ala sira uza buat ne'e, maibé ba saida, ami la hatene ona.'

Antropólogu ne'e halo tan viajen ida ba Oekusi hodi estuda oinsá ema halo rasik sira-nia *bano*, oinsá dansa sira ne'ebé uza *bano*, no saida mak dansa sira ne'e nia objetivu. Nia hanoin katak iha posibilidade boot katak *bano* Oekusi nian hanesan duni ho *bano* iha Xina nia muzeu. Komérsiu entre Xina ho Timor la'o dezde uluk liu, ho Xina nia hakarak mak foti ai-kameli no tinta naturál ba roupa. Parese ema Xina sira mak fó ka fa'an *bano* ba timoroan sira, no hatudo oinsá mak sira uza buat ne'e.

Iha Oekusi no Timor-Osidentál, ema hatudu dansa *bsoot*. Dansarinu sira uza *bano*, kanta no repete fraze badak ida ne'ebé kona malu di'ak ho ritmu ne'ebé múziku sira halo ho *sene* 6 ne'ebé tara, no *baba dook* ida ne'ebé hamriik ketak, ne'ebé akompaña dansarinu sira. Ema sira ne'e hotu tenke hamutuk iha ritmu nia laran atu dansa ne'e bele la'o kapás no sulin di'ak. *Bano* halo iha Pasabe, iha Oekusi nia foho ne'ebé besik fronteira ho Timor-Osidentál.

Bano ida nia tamañu mak sentímetru 2 X 1.5. Tali ida no au tubu ki'ik sira mak kesi sira hamutuk. Dansarinu kesi *bano* ba ain ida-idak. *Bano* ne'e todan: lahan ida nia todan mak entre kilograma 4 no 5.

Padre Richard Daschbach, ne'ebé halo knaar iha Kutet, Oekusi, promove kultura tradisionál durante tinan barak ona. Nia fó korajen ba labarik sira ne'ebé hela iha uma mahon Topu Honis atu dansa *bsoot* no uza *bano* alumíniu ne'ebé halo espesialmente duni ba labarik sira tanba alumíniu kmaan liu duké *bano* husi birak.

Dansarinu sira iha Suai Loro hatais *babuk* ne'ebé halo husi au. Sira nia lian mamar fali. *Ailoos* (xilofone ne'ebé hatuur iha ain leten) no *babuk* nia lian sei bele rona bainhira sira dansa.

EZEMPLU AUDIO *bsoot, bano, sene, ke'e* CD TRACK/FAIXA 8
EZEMPLU AUDIOVIZUÁL DVD SENA 7-12

Bsoot and Lelan

Although the general term for the foot-bell dance is *bsoot*, technically the word *bsoot* refers only to the step the men use. The men dance the *bsoot* by lifting one foot and stamping it, shuffling the other behind it, they must keep both feet moving all the time. However, one *bsoot* dancer who went to Jakarta with other proficients to give an exhibition of foot-bell dancing, hardly lifted his feet off the ground as he moved about, and he was doing the *bsoot*, not the *lelan* which is the women's version of the *bsoot*. The step the women do is less varied among individuals than the men's step, and has a distinctive shuffle-like quality to it. Usually the dancers of both the *bsoot* and *lelan* wear *bano* (heavy brass ankle-bells, or aluminium bells in recent times) but the dances do not have to be done with foot-bells. They can also be performed with chicken feathers tied to the feet, tufts of goat beard or palm leaves woven into cubes with pieces of wood inside each cube, which make a weak rattly sound as one dances.

These days the *bsoot* is a free-form dance, with each dancer creating his or her own individual style. In the past, the dance was more formal in structure and there were also different kinds of *bsoot*. The different types of leg-ware, as well as the different types of *bsoot*, have disappeared altogether. It is rumoured that there are pockets in other areas where some still remember how to dance the different types of *bsoot*, and sometimes still perform them. The *bsoot* is danced for all kinds of occasions, particularly celebrations such as weddings.

In 1981 the priest Richard Daschbach witnessed the more formal *bsoot* being performed in a part of Oekusi where very traditional culture was still observed, but never anywhere else since. The different types of leg-ware and different kinds of *bsoot* are well on their way into history books, where they will remain entombed both for the curious and for the serious student of past heritages.

In the *bsoot*, women beat the *sene* (gongs) - *sin nlekun sene* - 'they beat the gongs' and the *ke'e* (drum). The dancers follow the *sene*, not the ke'e. The ke'e is like the base drone of a bagpipe, adding body and atmosphere. The ke'e and sene can have a hypnotic effect on dancers, drummers and gong-beaters alike.

A visitor was once amused: the gongs and drum sounded like a cacophony to him, as the dancers milled about, not at all in unison. They stopped and told the gong beaters to get their act together, as they were out of rhythm. The women exchanged places and began again. It sounded even more cacophonous - but the dancers were now dancing in unison as if there was only one dancer. The gongs were now in the correct rhythm, even though the visitor's ear wasn't able to pick it out.[9]

As for the Chinese bells (thought to have originated from China) and the Timorese leg-ornaments, one could confidently postulate two possibilities. The first: Timor leg-ware came first, but the later Chinese bells were popular from the start. The second: the Chinese bells came first, but since they were expensive and difficult to procure, those who couldn't afford or even find a set resorted to other leg-ware.[10]

Bano

A cultural anthropologist once visited Oekusi and saw bano (ankle-bell) dancing. Upon inquiry he was told that no one knew where ankle-bells originated. He was intrigued but stymied. Later when he was traveling in Northern China he came across a museum and saw what looked like the same bells hanging there. He asked the curator about them and was told:

They were used by our ancestors thousands of years ago. In what way and for what purpose we no longer know.[11]

The anthropologist made his way back to Oekusi and studied how the ankle-bells were made locally, how they were affixed to the feet, what sort of dancing was done with them and for what purposes.

He assumed that since it is an established historical fact that there was extensive commerce for a long time between Timor and China (the Chinese being interested primarily in sandalwood and dyes) it was very likely the bells he saw in the museum were these self same bells. The Chinese would not only have sold or traded them to the Timorese, but would have shown them how they themselves used them and for what purposes.[12]

In Oekusi and West Timor the bsoot is also performed. The dancers wear the bano (brass ankle-bells - see previous page) and keep a rhythmic ostinato, interlocking with the rhythm being kept by the musicians playing the six hanging gongs and the free-standing goblet drum which accompanies the dancers. They must all keep strict time together for the dance to be fluid and continuous.

The bano are made in Pasabe, a remote village in the mountains of Oekusi, near the border of West Timor. They are about 1.5 cm x 2 cm in size and are threaded together on a length of palm twine with bamboo connector tubes (about 0.5 cm in diameter and 2 cm in length). The dancer wraps the strand of bells around each ankle. They are very heavy - each strand has about 24 bells on it and weighs 4 to 5 kilograms.

The priest in Kutet, Father Richard Daschbach, has been a champion for the promotion of the traditional culture of Oekusi for many years, actively encouraging the children in his care to dance and sing traditional music. The children in the Topu Honis orphanage and safe house (Kutet, Oekusi) dance the bsoot using aluminium bano that Father Dashbach commissioned from bell makers especially for children, since they are much lighter than the brass bano. The dancers of the bidu ailoos in Suai Loro, Kovalima wear bamboo ankle-bells called babuk. The babuk have a much softer sound.

AUDIO EXAMPLE of bsoot/bano/sene/ke'e CD TRACK 8
AUDIO VISUAL EXAMPLE DVD SCENES 7-12

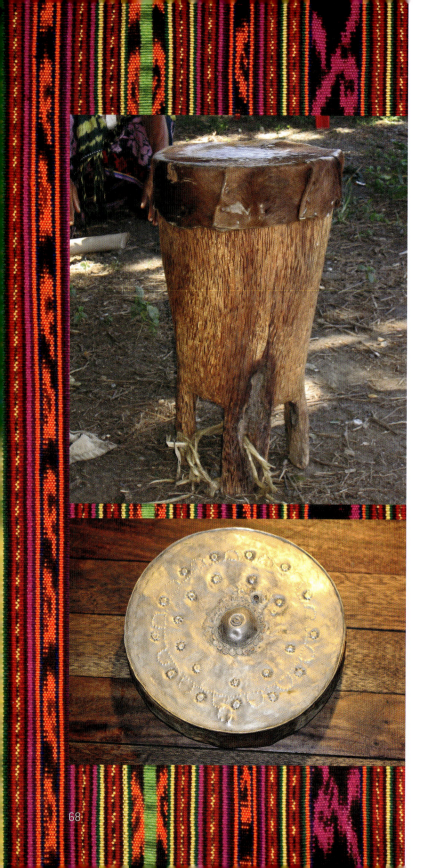

Ke'e

Ke'e ne'e hamriik mesak ho ain haat no iha isin kuhus. *Ke'e* ita bele hetan iha Oekusi no Timor-Osidentál, toka hamutuk ho *leku sene* hodi akompaña *bsoot*. Feto na'in haat tu'ur haleu nia no dere hamutuk. Feto ida mak fai batar ka foos ho lailais no ritmu kontinua nafatin no la troka, no ritmu sira ne'e hanesan improvizasaun de'it. Bainhira nia kole, seluk troka ninia fatin, no sira kontinua nafatin. *Ke'e* ne'ebé di'ak liu halo husi nuu-hun, ho *ke'e* ulun halo husi kulit husi karau-timur ka karau-baka ne'ebé sira estika tiha. *Ke'e* nia aas entre sentímetru 50-55, ho diámetru maizumenus sentímetru 35.

EZEMPLU AUDIO *ke'e* CD TRACK / FAIXA 8
EZEMPLU AUDIOVIZUÁL DVD SENA 7-12

Sene

Iha Oekusi, konjuntu *sene* mak bolu *in leku sene* iha lian Baikeno. Ne'e la uza melodia, no toka hodi akompaña dansa *bsoot*. In leku signifika katak 'nia (feto) dere.' Bele mós uza iha situasaun seluk. *Tala* sira ne'e ita bolu *sene*, ne'ebé iha *sene* 5 tara husi riin ida, ne'ebé feto na'in 3 mak toka. Ida premeiru mak ki'ik liu (ho lian aas) bolu *toluk*. Ida ne'e mak hahú dansa, fó ritmu, determina ninia lais, no bolu bainhira atu para, konforme oinsá tokadór baku nia. Tuir mai iha *tala* rua naran *teufnaij* ne'ebé mós tara, ida iha leten, ida iha kraik. Normalmente dansarinu sira dansa tuir *teufnaij*.

Tala rua ikus nian mak naran *kbola*, ita tara *tala* sira ne'e ho pozisaun vertikál teten malu. *Tala* sira ne'e nia tamañu boot liu duké *teufnaij* no sai mós nu'udar baixu. Ita dere *tala* sira ne'e ho ritmu 2/8 ne'ebé lailais.

Jeralmente, dansarinu sira dansa tuir *teufnaij*. Maibé, se karik ema ne'ebé dere *teufnaij* dere ladún maka'as kompara ho *tala* sira seluk, dansarinu sira sei dansa tuir *kbola*, ka *toluk*. Dansarinu sira ne'ebé uza *bano* tenke dansa tuir *sene*. Se lae, dala ruma sira-nia xefe sei siak. Bainhira sira dansa tuir *sene*, son sira kordena malu di'ak no bele halo rona na'in sira sente dukur ka ipnotiza tiha.

EZEMPLU AUDIO *bsoot/bano/sene/ke'e* CD TRACK/FAIXA 8
EZEMPLU AUDIOVIZUÁL DVD SENA 7-12

Ke'e

Ke'e is the freestanding, four-legged, single-headed conical drum found in Oekusi and West Timor and is played with the gong ensemble, the *leku sene*, to accompany the *bsoot*. It is played by four women, who squat around the drum. One woman pounds with a fast repetitive beat, without any set rhythm. When she is tired, this is usually after a short while, another takes over and so on. The best *ke'e* is made of coconut wood, with the skin of cow or buffalo stretched across the drumhead. It stands at approximately 50 - 55 cm, with a diameter of approximately 35 cm.

Sene

In Oekusi, the gong ensemble is called *sene* (Baikeno). It is non-melodic and is played to accompany the *bsoot*. *In leku* means, she beats. It can also be used in other contexts. The gongs themselves are simply called *sene*. *Sene* consists of five hanging gongs on a vertical beam, played by three women. The first, which is also the smallest (and so the highest in pitch), is called *toluk*. This starts the dance, gives the rhythm, sets the pace and calls the halts, all by the way it is beaten. The next two gongs, hanging vertically one above the other, are called collectively *teufnaij*. They are the ones the dancers generally follow.

The final two gongs, also hanging vertically one above the other, are called *kbola*. These are bigger than the *teufnaij* and so have a deeper bass quality. The gongs are beaten in 2/8 time and play in rapid rhythm.

Dancers generally follow the middle set of gongs, the *teufnaij*. However, if the *teufnaij* player is not beating as hard as the other gong players, or if the sound of the *teufnaij* does not carry, dancers will follow the *kbola*, or even the *toluk*. Dancers with *bano* are expected to follow the *sene*, and are sometimes reprimanded if they don't. When they do, the co-ordinated sounds of *sene*, *ke'e* and *bano* is very hypnotic.

AUDIO EXAMPLE *bsoot/bano/sene/ke'e* **CD TRACK 8**
AUDIO VISUAL EXAMPLE DVD SCENES 7-12

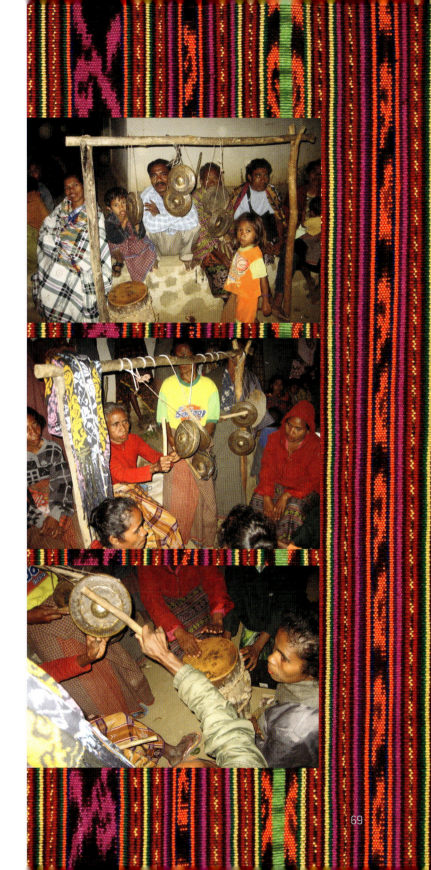

Bonet

Bonet ne'e dansa sírkulu Meto nian ne'ebé halo ho sani poezia klasikál. Ninia hakat no liafuan diferente iha fatin ida ba fatin seluk. Iha fatin balu partisipante sira tau liman ba ninia maluk nia kabaas, kanta, no muda tuir sírkulu maibé ho diresaun 'kontra oras.' Iha fatin seluk, sira hamriik rabat malu, kabaas kona kabaas kuandu halo sírkulu. Iha fatin seluk tan, dansarinu sira tama no sai husi sírkulu nia klaran. Sira-nia hakat ne'e komplikadu liu duké hakat sírkulu simplis ida.

Bonet ne'e kompostu husi *sit* (knananuk) no *nel* (sani). *Nel* mak apresentasaun liu husi dansa no kanta, kona-ba moris Meto nian. *Nel* ne'e preserva poezia meto antigu nian ne'ebé ema sani tuir ezaktamente, dezde uluk kedas. Ohin loron ema Meto rasik ladún komprende ona liafuan antigu sira ne'ebé sei repete nafatin to'o agora.

Iha tempu uluk, *nel* ne'e apresenta de'it husi *tobe ida* (ema ne'ebé mak iha papél atu tau matan ba tradisaun no serve nu'udar lider serimónia). Uluk liu *nel* ne'e apresenta de'it ba liurai sira maibé neneik neneik, ba ema hotu. Bainhira *nel* tun ba nivel povu baibain nian, tuir istória katak iha fatin ida, lia na'in tenke kompete ho lia na'in seluk. Ida mak halo *nel* ida mak hanesan kódigu ne'ebé lia na'in seluk tenke koko atu deskobre, no esplika ninia signifikadu, uza hela poezia ne'ebé nia inventa iha tempu ne'e kedas. Dala barak *nel* halo espesialmente ba loron boot ruma ho intensaun atu konfundi ekipa seluk, atu sira labele deskobre no esplika kódigu. Dala ruma, ekipa ne'ebé la konsege deskobre kódigu ida tenke selu multa boot. Ohin loron, ekipa ida ne'ebé lakon tenke sosa tua ba ekipa ne'ebé manán.

Bonet antigu ne'e hatudu ona sinál katak nia bele lakon husi mundu.

Sani ne'e kompostu husi knananuk badak (segundu 10-15) sira ne'ebé la muda. Versu istória iha 15-20 versu badak sira, ida-idak nia durasaun maizumenus segundu tolu de'it. Versu sira ne'e bolu 'nel.' Ema ne'ebé mak lidera bolu Akón nel. Nia hamriik nu'udar parte sírkulu nian iha knua balu no iha klaran, mesak, iha fatin balu tan. Nia bele inventa rasik ninia versu istória, maibé tenke halo ho poezia klasikál. Ohin loron ema uitoan de'it mak halo hanesan ne'e. Iha *bonet*, liafuan mak importante, la'os melodia.

Sírkulu *bonet* fahe ba parte rua ne'ebé kanta parte rua ne'ebé ketak maibé hatutan malu (maksani ida seidauk remata ninia versaun bainhira maksani seluk repete filafali saida mak nia rona husi maksani ne'ebé lidera). Akón nel sei hakilar versu *nel* ida. Sírkulu nia seksaun premeiru hahú *sit* ida no hatama versu ne'e iha *sit* nia laran. Molok sira remata, seksaun segundu hahú *sit* seluk tan maibé la hatama versu ruma. Molok seksaun segundu remata, Akón nel bolu ona versu seluk ne'ebé tuir mai. Buat ne'e la'o nune'e ba nafatin. Bainhira versu/istória hotu ona, Akón nel sei fó hatene liu husi versu badak ida. Ne'e mak kantiga badak ida hananu hamutuk para ema hotu hatene katak *nel* (versu/istória) remata tiha ona. Kantiga ne'e bolu: "O nunuh matau toel." Entaun Akón nel sani versu rua hodi remata. Hafoin versu ida, seksaun rua sani: "Hainu kolo liu soe," hatama hela versu finál nian rua. Ne'e mak bonet *nel* remata. Seluk tan bele hahú.

Ezemplu bonet ida bele kanta hanesan tuir mai ne'e:

Akón nel: O pipje natau maun

Seksaun dahuluk husi sírkulu kanta:

Hainu kolo liu soe, akakoe, o - le -ane,
O pipje nat au maun,nu-u laleok, behe na se,
sin he nkaen, nkaen kolo la liu soe
Molok atu remata, seksaun daruak hahú nune'e:

O lilo maun, e maun ana, e, e-e-sa-se,
paleo he nkae, nkae kolo la liu soe

Seksaun daruak ne'e la hatama versu, no antes sira remata, Akón nel sei bolu versu ne'ebé tuir mai, no kontinua hanesan ne'e.

Versu sira husi kualker *nel* bele hatama iha kualker *sit*, no *sit* ne'e uza ate *nel* ne'e remata. *Sit toben* mak kanta husi sírkulu sorin balu parte segundu nian. Kualker *sit* bele uza iha ne'e, no normalmente *sit* ida mak kanta durante *nel* tomak.

Ritmu versu *nel* nian (no mós *sit* nian) mak 2/2, ne'ebé sustenta liu husi hatama liafuan badak ne'ebé la iha signifikadu. "O" premeiru iha *nel* balu la'os tama iha ritmu. Nia pronúnsia ho lian aas, no serve nu'udar entrada ba versu ne'ebé tuir nia. Porezemplu:

Akón nel: O/ pipje nat au maun

Koru: O/pi-ip-je na-ta-u-u maun

Akón nel: O/ bati fai fai

Koru: O/ba-a-ti fai, je-e-en fai

Iha realidade, parte ki'ik balu sei la pronúnsia sai, liuliu hafoin hemu tua kopu ida ka rua.

Bonet ne'ebé di'ak sei mantein nafatin ritmu ipnótiku.

Akón nel ne'ebé di'ak sei halo *nel* sira troka nafatin, no bolu sira tuir orden ne'ebé iha. Membru sira iha koru sei maizumenus hatene *nel* sira ho di'ak, maibé sira la domina matéria ne'e natoon atu sai Akón nel.

Bonet

The *bonet* is the Metonese circle dance performed while chanting classical poetry. The step and chants differ from place to place. In some places the participants lay their arms across one another's shoulders and sing as they move slowly around in a circle in an anti-clockwise direction. In other places they stand shoulder to shoulder as they encircle. In yet other places they move in and out, toward and away, from the centre of the circle as they encircle. Their step is a bit more complicated than the simple circle step.

The *bonet* is made up of *sits* (songs) and *nels* (chants). *Nels* are a presentation in dance and song form of some facet of Metonese life. *Nels* preserve ancient Metonese poetry, which, as it has been repeated verbatim through the centuries, is now mostly unintelligible to modern Metonese, even though they continue to repeat it verbatim.

In ancient times, *nels* were recited, (in royal circles first, then it filtered down to everyone) only by the *tobe* (custodian of tradition and functioning as ceremonial priest). When it filtered down to local *adat* (priests) and *adat* (heads - the two are not the same) the story goes, in one area, that formerly *adat* and *adat* would compete with other *adat* and *adat*. One would compose a *nel* in the highly figurative, compressed (coded) language common to the genre. His competitor would have to "crack" the code and expound its meaning, also in verse. *Nels* were often made up for the occasion, and were geared to "tie up," that is, confound the ones designated to answer. There were sometimes heavy fines for failing to crack a *nel*. Nowadays, if one party "ties up" another party by reciting a set *nel* - which requires another set *nel* to "untie themselves" - and they forget it, they have to buy *tua* (alcoholic) drink for the other party. The *tua* will be readily available nearby.[13]

The chant consists of set songs that don't change and are 10 to 15 seconds in length. The verse-story consists of 15 to 20 short verses, each a few seconds in duration. The verse-story or any of its verses are called *nel*. A caller is the *Akón nel*, who is part of the circle in some areas, while in other places he stands in the middle of the circle by himself. A verse-caller may compose his own verse-story, but would be expected to do so in the genre of classical poetry. Few would do so now. The focus of the *bonet* is on the words not the melody.

The *bonet* circle is divided into two sections that overlap whilst singing. The *Akón nel* calls out a verse of a *nel*. The first section of the circle starts a *sit* and inserts the verse into it. Before they are finished, the second section of the circle begins another *sit*, and finishes it without inserting any verse. The *Akón nel* is already calling out the next verse before the second group has finished, and so on. When the verse-story is finished the *Akón nel* will say so in a short verse. Then a short chant is sung together so everyone knows the *nel* (verse-story) is over. The chant is called: *O nunuh matau toel*. Then the *Akón nel* intones the two set closing verses.

After each verse both halves of the circle sing a set chant: *Hainu kolo liu soe*, putting the two closing verses into this chant one by one. The *bonet nel* is now finished. Another one may be started.

An example of how a *bonet* might be sung is as follows:

Akón nel : *O pipje natau maun*

First section of the circle sings:

Hainu kolo liu soe, akakoe, o - le -ane,
O pipje nat au maun, nu-u laleok, behe na se,
sin he nkaen, nkaen kolo la liu soe

Before they are finished, the second circle begins:

O lilo maun, e maun ana, e, e-e-sa-se,
paleo he nkae, nkae kolo la liu soe

This second circle doesn't insert any verse into it and before they have finished the Akón nel calls out the next verse, and so on.

Verses of a particular *nel* can be inserted into any *sit*, and the same *sit* is used during the entire *nel*. The *sit toben*, or covering song, is sung by the second half of the circle. This can also be any *sit*, and usually the same *sit* is sung during the entire *nel*.

The rhythm of a *nel* verse (and of the *sit*) is 2/2. It is maintained by inserting meaningless syllables when needed, or by glottal stops on a particular vowel. The initial "O" present in some *nels*, isn't part of the rhythm. It is pronounced in a higher, lengthened tone, as though leading into the verse it precedes.

For example:

Akón nel: O/ pipje nat au maun

Chanters: O/pi-ip-je na-ta-u-u maun

Akón nel: O/ bati fai fai

Chanters: O/ba-a-ti fai, je-e-en fai

In practice, the glottal stops will not always be clearly enunciated, especially after a cup or two of the *tua* brew.

A good *bonet* will keep to the hypnotic rhythm.

A good *Akón nel* will keep the *nels* moving, and call them in order. Most of the chanters know some or most of the *nels* to some extent, but not enough to become *Akón nel*.

Sadly, the ancient *bonet* is showing all the signs of being a dying form of art.

AUDIO EXAMPLE *of the bonet* **CD TRACK 22**
AUDIO VISUAL EXAMPLE **DVD SCENES 7-12**

Bonet Sit Ualu

1 O lilo maun, e maun ana, e, e-e-sa se,
  pale he nkae, nkae kolo la liu soe

  Manu ki'ik ida, husik nia tanis... seluk labele komprende

2 Hainu kolo liu soe, akakoe, o-le-ane, nu-u laleok,
  behe-na-se, sin he nkaen, nkaen kolo la liu soe
  - labele komprende

3 O feku bati feuk, se-e-le-mau, o-la-a mau, au-u tili tae, o-o-o-le
  - feku flauta... seluk labele komprende

4 O he le la, koa he le tebes e se-le-na-ma
  e-hé-ama, o hó-o hé-e-lé-e-la
  - labele komprende

5 O-he pe, he le lu-u-at aum a he ta-saun, teuba hai noel,
  noel a lu-u-at, seola hai moekta, o he-pe, he-le lu-u-at tu
  - noel- mota / seluk la komprende

6 O kolo laku lilo oef, o-o-eb lilo, lilo he le-e-na no,
  ba-ha-a-na, he hama ba-e, o-o-o-le
  kolo-manu / lilo=sinál alein de ne'e labele komprende

7 O fatu bena til, ba-ha-a boek, se-he-na-ne
  he hau po-a, ne-e ka-bol, ano-e muit, sa-a-na-ne

  Fatu bena= fatuk belar. Hau poa = ai hun nia kulit
  Mu'it = karau

8 Hama-u-bae, o-o-o-le, a-ka-a-koe, na-a-na-ne
  O-le-a-ne, nu-nu-o-ma, ta-ah a-toe, se-e-na-ne
  - labele komprende

Sani Tipu Bonet Seluk Tan

Muiskatele

Ne'e mak sani oan ida ne'ebé hanesan *bonet*, maibé kanta iha to'os laran bainhira fokit du'ut aat sira. Knaar ne'e halo dala rua, normalmente iha Janeiru, konforme udan.

Nel sira no sani sira diferente husi *bonet* maibé husi inan ida de'it. Diferensa mak iha *bonet* ema halo forma sírkulu maibé iha *muiskatele* partisipante sira fokit hela du'ut aat. Ohin loron ema barak liu mak la halo ona *muiskatele*, no fokit du'ut aat nonok de'it.

Oebani

Ne'e sani oan ida ne'ebé halo bainhira kesi batar hodi halo ai-selat no kabutu, mak tara iha uma kabuar, iha ahi-matan nia leten atu hamenus fuhuk sira. *Oebani nel* sira la hanesan ho *bonet* no *muiskatele nel* sira. Ohin loron ema hahú atu haluhan *oebani nel* sira.

Pankalalále

Ne'e mós sani oan iha *bonet* nia família, kanta iha mate uma molok atu hakoi mate-isin. Ema sira ne'ebé prepara foos atu tein hodi fó ba bainaka sira maka kanta *pankalalále*. Sani ne'e diferente iha fatin fatin no mós diferente ohin no aban, maski ema ne'ebé hanesan mak kanta. Versaun ida ne'e mak hateten sai ba Richard Daschbach atu hakerek, husi Tia Pasquela Eko. Nia kuaze mesak mak hatene iha Kutet nia laran, no kada vez nia kanta, *pankalalále* ne'e diferente.

EZEMPLU AUDIO *Pankalalále* CD TRACK/FAIXA 33
EZEMPLU AUDIOVIZUÁL DVD SENA 7-12

Pankalalále

o le manu nani ko beti
maun belu ba,
e maun sa la la, la la la la.

Seiki nameu na man,
ai manu nako nai jan.
Pankalalále nao nako me,
nao nako ia ma-o ma-e.
La le mulai hau bakan fi la le i.

Lolu ak lolou, i ho-e,
le bae toli kaisla ho-e,
lou lou ak ko san.
Sala nunbai tunan.
Tun ana le mumnau nekma bae.
Le bae toli kase,
le bau toli kaesle hais e nuen.

Lou-lou ak sa,
ahoe, kita le kol, akbali bae.
Sala nunbae tunan
tun ama mumnau nekat bae
Mnao kum bae, mfain kum bae, sia la sia le lo hai on i.

Husi kolo husi kolo lo ri ri kolo bae.
O ri ri ri hai dober bae, hai dober bae.
Bani bani sae bi sol-solo bae, solo bae.
Bani bani sae bi sol-solo bae, solo bae.

O ra ri kakoe, seik-seiki jambua no'o bae,
tabua ba mabe mese.
Le e la le, e la le ei la lei e la lei aloi ho-e hau.
O le e sa kita kolo kol sai alumta bae.

Pankalalále e i
a le manu nani ko beti,
o le o le manu nani ko senu,
o a o le, o le a talei ka koe.
E maun belu ba, e maun sa la la, la la la la.
Seiki nameu na man,
ai manu nako naijan.
Pankalalále nao nako me, nao nako i ma o ma e,
la le mulai hau bakan la le i.
Mnao kum bae, mfain kum bae,
sia la sia le lo hai on i.

Eight Bonet Sit

1 O lilo maun, e maun ana, e, e-e-sa se,
   pale he nkae, nkae kolo la liu soe

   - A little chicken, let it cry... the rest, unintelligible

2 Hainu kolo liu soe, akakoe, o-le-ane, nu-u laleok,
   behe-na-se, sin he nkaen, nkaen kolo la liu soe
   - unintelligible

3 O feku bati feuk, se-e-le-mau, o-la-a mau, au-u tili tae, o-o-o-le
   - *feku* - flute... the rest, unintelligible

4 O he le la, koa he le tebes e se-le-na-ma
   e-hé-ama, o hó-o hé-e-lé-e-la
   - unintelligible

5 O-he pe, he le lu-u-at aum a he ta-saun, teuba hai noel,
   noel a lu-u-at, seola hai moekta, o he-pe, he-le lu-u-at tu
   - *noel* = river... the rest, unintelligible

6 O kolo laku lilo oef, o-o-eb lilo, lilo he le-e-na no,
   ba-ha-a-na, he hama ba-e, o-o-o-le
   kolo = bird *lilo* = sign... the rest, unintelligible

7 O fatu bena til, ba-ha-a boek, se-he-na-ne
   he hau po-a, ne-e ka-bol, ano-e muit, sa-a-na-ne

   - Fatu bena = flat rock Hau poa = bark of tree
   mu'it = cattle... the rest, unintelligible

8 Hama-u-bae, O-O-O-le, a-ka-a-koe, na-a-na-ne
   O-le-a-ne, nu-nu-o-ma, ta-ah a-toe, se-e-na-ne
   - unintelligible

Other Bonet-genre Chants

Muiskatele

This is *bonet*-type chanting, sung in the gardens whilst doing the weeding. Gardens are weeded twice, usually in January, depending on when the fickle rainy season begins. The *nels* and chants are different from the *bonets*, but of the same genre. The difference between *bonet* and *muiskatele* is that the *bonet* participants move in a circle, while the *muiskatele* participants weed as they chant. Many people today have lost the *muiskatele* and just weed without chanting.

Oebani

A *bonet*-genre chanting is also done while tying harvested corn into *aisat* and *kabutu*, to be hung over the cooking area in the round houses for smoking to keep down the corn weevil. The *oebani nels* and chants differ from *bonet* and *muiskatele nels* and chants. Nowadays people are beginning to forget the *oebani nels*.

Pankalalále

The *pankalalále* is another *bonet*-genre chant, sung at the home of a deceased person before their burial. Rice provided as part of the funeral meal for guests after burial is pounded in a *lesun* (mortar). As it is pounded the *pankalalále* is chanted. The chant is different in different areas and even with performance to performance sung by the same person.

The version on the previous page is of the *pankalalále* as dictated to Richard Daschbach. Sung by Pasquela Eko, one of the few people in Kutet who knows the chant, this version was also different each time she sang it.

AUDIO EXAMPLE of *Pankalalále* **CD TRACK 33**
AUDIO VISUAL **DVD SCENES 7-12**

NEL LIMA

Nel mak apresentasaun dansa no hananu kona-ba moris ema Meto nian. Uluk, *nel* só kanta ba liurai sira, maibé liutiha sékulu barak, ema baibain foti *nel* nu'udar sira-nia eransa komún.

Poezia tuan husi *nel* no *sit* sira ne'e iha forma ida ne'ebé loke posibilidade atu halo tradusaun ka interpretasaun oioin. Nune'e iha similaridade ho estilu hakerek Xina nian. Karakter Xina nian ida kompostu husi parte parte ne'ebé sujere signifikadu la'os fó duni signifikadu. Maski nune'e ema Xina ohin loron komprende ho signifikadu husi liafuan sira ne'e. Parte parte *nel* no *sit* nian mós sujere de'it signifikadu, tamba sira badak demais atu halo buat seluk. Ema Meto sira ohin loron barak liu la hatene ezatamente saida mak signifika *nel* no *sit*.

A *nel* is a presentation in dance and song form of some facet of Metonese life. *Nels* were originally sung only in royal circles, but in time appropriated by their subjects as their common heritage.

The ancient poetry of these *nels* and *sits* is grammatically and syntactically trimmed and cut, making it susceptible to a number of translations. In this respect, the *nels* resemble Chinese characters. The different parts of a particular character only suggest, rather than give meaning. However the modern Chinese knows what that meaning is. The different parts of a Metonese *nel* or *sit* only suggest, rather than give meaning (they are too short and pared down to do otherwise). Unlike his counterpart in China, the modern Metonese doesn't know with certainty the meaning of much or most of the *nels* and *sits*.

1 O hai aim mitnin
2 O bi nine fai fai
   O kaslul sa-an
   O slulu boen hele
   O Usi boen hele
3 O tite faij mese
4 O bati fai-fai
   O oinje npipis
   O pipse nat-au maun
   O pipse nat-au tuan
5 O tuan-e-maun-Benu
6 O tuan-e Uis maun Benu
7 O in on lite
8 O litje at au pah
9 O litje at au tob
   (O au ak on i naleok ai ka a-ka-koe) *optional*

Mai hodi rona
Iha kalan boot

Dudu ba kotuk kalan ida tan...
(seluk la iha signifikadu)
Fahe nia hodi sai kalan sira

Xefe boot mak Señor Benu
Xefe boot mak Xefe aas Señor Benu
Nia hanesan goma
Nia mak halo rai metin
Nia mak hametin ema nia relasaun ba malu

O come and hear
In the night time

O push it off at night... [rest unintelligible]
O divide it into nights... [rest unintelligible]

The lord is Sir Benu
The lord is the high lord Sir Benu
He's like glue (i.e. like a bond)
He glues (bonds) the land together
He glues (bonds) the people together

Nel sira sempre remata ho buat ne'ebé tuir mai ne'e:

O neu teuf kaun molo   (*Sit Hainu kolo liu soe* – sempre uza ba ida ne'e)
O kanbe't pal-pala   (a iha buat ida ne'ebé atu hatama iha versu rua ne'ebé taka)
O neu teuf kaun molo   *Kaun molo* = ular samodok (alein de ne'e, la iha signifikadu)
O kanbe 't pal pala   Naran ne'e badak duni – ita to'o ona ba nia rohan

Nels are always closed with the following:

O neu teuf kaun molo   (the *sit - Hainu kolo liu soe* - is always used for this)
O kanbe't pal-pala   (Nothing is inserted into these two closing verses, neither is there a "covering song")
O neu teuf kaun molo   *Kaun molo* = yellow snake [Rest meaningless]
O kanbe 't pal pala   The name is very short - we've come to the end

NOTA *Nel* ida-idak hakerek ho kór tuir mai: Baikeno - matak, Tetun - metan, English -malahuk. 'Labele komprende' iha ne'e refere ba faktu ida katak linguajen *nel* if sira nian mak iha dalen meto klasikál, ne'ebé kuaze ema hotu la hatene ona. Tinan ba tinan, ema aprende *nel* sira liu husi repete tuir de'it, no ninia signifikadu balu lakon.

NOTE The language of each *nel* is represented as follows: Baikeno - green, Tetun - black and English - grey. Unintelligible means, in this context, that the language of the *nels* is often classical Metonese which most people no longer speak or understand. Verses have been learnt and sung verbatim through the centuries and have lost their meaning.

O au tem nin molo O molo hai kopas O kopse nkoit sasi	*Nel* ida ne'e kolia kona-ba liurai rai tetuk nian, reinu da Costa nian	This *nel* speaks of the king of the lowlands, the da Costa dynasty
O sasi ma nak isu O isben nafek sala O au sal non mese	(la komprende mak barak)	(mostly unintelligible)
O tupuk neu Bihenu	tupuk = butuk	*tupuk* = a pile of
O tupuk neu Bisono O tupuk neu Bikusi O ai Bihenu tabal-bal	Bihenu ba nafatin, kadunan liurai Benu originál nian	*bihenu* is forever; the palace of the original King Benu
O ai Bisono tama ma'i	Bisono iha ne'e agora; kadunan da Costa nian husi nusa Solor	*bisono* is here now; the palace of the da Costas from the island of Solor
O ai Bikusi senu-sekal O he taseun i-i-i seka O tamel bet nub	Oekusi, troka malu... (labele komprende)	The town of Oekusi... exchange... (unintelligible)
O nok nain bien, bien 't nino Kosat	Ita hela ho balu, seluk da Costa nian; liurai Benu tuan ne'e la lakon	We keep some, the rest is da Costa's, i.e: the old King Benu doesn't disappear for good
O in on a-a-a lite, litje nat au pah	Nia hanesan goma, halo rai metin	He's a bond, bonding the land
O in on a-a-a lite, litje nat au tob	Nia hanesan goma, halo ema nia relasaun metin	He's a bond, bonding the people

NOTA Liurai orijinál husi Ambenu mak Ama Benu ne'ebé mós iha apelidu da Cruz. Nia hanesan fundadór ba luta hasoru ukun Portugál nian maizumenus iha tinan 1800. Portugál sira mak manán, entaun Ama Benu halai tiha ba Timor-Osidentál, fatin ne'ebé ninia bei-oan sira sei hela to'o agora. Portugál hili família foun, da Costa sira, ne'ebé uluk mai Oekusi nu'udar negosiante sira. Maibé, tuir povo nia hanoin, da Costa sira só ukun rai tetuk ne'ebé inklui Pante Makasaar. Ama Benu ne'ebé halai tiha mak konsidera nu'udar liurai ba foho (Ambenu nia rai barak liu mak iha foho leten) no mós ba ema Meto orijinál ne'ebé ema foho.

NOTE The original king of Ambenu was Ama Benu who also has the name da Cruz. He initiated the Ambenu revolt against the Portuguese in the early nineteenth century. The Portuguese won, and so Ama Benu fled to West Timor, where his descendants still live. Portugal appointed a new dynasty, the da Costas, who originally came to Oekusi as businessmen. However in the peoples' mind, the da Costas were rulers only of the lowlands where the town of Oekusi is located. The exiled Ama Benu was regarded as the king of the mountains (Ambenu is mostly mountain) and of the original Metonese mountain people.[14]

NEL NÚMERU TOLU	SIGNIFIKADU NEL NÚMERU TOLU	NEL THREE
O uis boen hele, tite faij mese	*Nel* ida ne'e kolia sobre roupa ne'ebé mane sira	This *nel* speaks of the clothes men
O bati fai-fai	(beti) no feto sira (tais) hatais	(the *beti*) and women (the *tais*) wear
Tamaub tais beti	ó-nia beti no tais bosan ona	You wear out your *beti* and *tais*
Mite mu sa-sa?	Agora hanusa?	Now what?
Tais i mutai sa?	Agora hanusa?	What's next?
Ni abse moni	Kabas moris	The cotton grows
Monik haube kun	Ó dada nia (hodi halo kabas talin)	You draw it out (to make thread)
Teli takbali	Ó dada nia hodi halo kabas talin	You make balls of thread
Mitais 'm beti	Ó halo tais no beti barak	You make *taises* and *betis*
Bet nim bose	Beti mak tipu orijinál (husi kabas ne'ebé halo rasik iha uma)	The *beti* is the original type (of home-spun cotton)
Bafe lo'e natun	(labele komprende)	(unintelligible)
Tai fut kase	Tais ne'e husi mafutar ne'ebé sosa iha loja	The *tais* is store-bought patterns
Boke lo'e natun	(labele komprende)	(unintelligible)
Ni akon i	(labele komprende)	(unintelligible)
Tuaf kon molo	(labele komprende)	(unintelligible)
Kanbe pal-pala	Ita to'o ona. . . tempu atu remata	We've come to the end
Meik 't mutai mana nau	Foti ida ne'e no hare'e tok saida mak ó bele halo ho nia	Take this and see what you can do with it

NEL NÚMERU HAAT	SIGNIFIKADU NEL NÚMERU HAAT	NEL FOUR
O maeb mesi i	Ohin kalan	Tonight
Neu meob es nem	Bainaka ida mai tiha ona	A knight (guest) has arrived
Nem 't ma'oe solo	Sira mai atu... (seluk la komprende)	They come to... the rest unintelligible
Neu mat mesokan	Ba matan nakukun, ita la koñese sira (hanesan poezia)	To darkened eyes, ie, we don't know them (poetic)
Okne ka manhinen	Ita la koñese sira	We don't know them
Au fe maspe'u	Ha'u sei matan dukur	I'm still sleepy-eyed
Neu kabuk no'o	Lori kabuka tahan mai (ai-moruk matan nian)	Bring *kabuka* tree leaves (an eye medication)
Sasaop kau mat ak	Kose ha'u-nia matan	Brush my eyes (with it)
Au matke nme'u	Ha'u hare'e moos ona	My eyes are (now) clear
Uhin ani	Ha'u koñese sira	I know (recognise them)
Bi (insert name) tuakini	Ne'e (tau naran iha ne'e) nia grupu	It's the group of (insert name)
Naok man kau, au kaeb lo'et nem	Dudu ha'u bá, tamba kohe bua-malus iha ne'e hela	Sweep me along, for the betel-nut purse is here
Ok meonbe mnainbe malo'en	Ita sei mama, hamutuk ho bainaka sira	We're going to chew it together with the guests
Au lo'e utes an ko Bi (insert name)	Ha'u sei lolo ba ó	I'll pass it around to you, - insert name
Akalke mam,sa le'e ni es	Kohe-mama hale'u sírkulu	The purse goes around
Lof ka lo'e fa, saseol fut manu	Maibé la'os kohe ne'e, maibé *nel* ne'e	But it's not the purse, it's this *nel*
Lof mutfek manu, main alo le'u	Bainhira ó silu tiha nia, halai dook tiha ba tempu badak	When you snap it , run off a bit
Fain oum main, sae liol belan	Bainhira ó filafali mai, *nel* ne'e hotu ona	When you come back, the *nel* is over
Bel namkesin, kesin ko Bi (insert name)	*Nel* ne'e hotu, ó simu ona nu'udar bainaka	The *nel* is over, you're received as a guest

Nel ida ne'e hodi simu bainaka sira. Sira 'futu tiha' iha laran, no presiza sani *nel* seluk tan atu kore an. Sira sala karik mak sira tenke selu multa (ohin loron, tua ba ema hotu).

Ema ka grupu ne'ebé 'futu' ho *nel* tenke liberta an husi *nel* ne'e liu husi sani *nel* seluk ne'ebé 'hatán' ba nia. Resposta ne'e bele deskobre kódigu ka ai-sasi'ik ne'ebé iha, ka, hanesan ema halo ohin loron, bele sani nel ne'ebé baibain serve nu'udar resposta.

This fourth *nel* receives guests. They are "tied up" in it, and have to recite another *nel* to extricate themselves. If they fail, they have to pay a fine (nowadays, some tua drink for everybody). When you extricate yourselves from our *nel*, retire to rest up, as you've just arrived from a distance.

To "tie up" the person or group by use of a *nel*, obliges them then to disengage from that *nel* by using another *nel* that "answers" it. The "answer" would be either decoding the original riddle encoded in it, or, as is done nowadays, by reciting a standard answer *nel*.[15]

NEL NÚMERU LIMA	SIGNIFIKADU NEL LIMA	NEL FIVE
Mitnin kit kol fai-faije	Rona ba manu kalan nia lian	Listen to the night bird calling
In he nkae tatek sekau kanan	Nia bolu sé nia naran?	It's calling out whose name
Ntek nates, tesan ko Bi	Nia haleu fatin ne'e, no mai tuur iha ó	It makes the rounds, and lands on you
Lof main koit, minouf ko Bi	Se karik ó hakat ba kotuk, ami sei hatún ó	If you back off, we'll bring you down
Haek ain to'an, uteut ko Bi	Tuba rai metin no ami sei ajuda ó hamriik	Stand your ground and we'll prop you up
Bi ----he nmouf, nabet on manu	Ó monu karik, ó sei tebe hanesan manu ne'ebé oho tiha	If you fall, you'll kick like a slaughtered chicken
Maeb me i, oum he simbe lo'et	Orasida kalan, mai foti ó-nia osan	This evening, come get your pay
Lo'e nis kau, utua toeb ko sa	Ó oferta bua-malus, ha'u sei fó fali saida?	You offer me the betel-nut, I'll pay back with what?
Utua san neuba naijan knit hu'e	(labele komprende)	(unintelligible)
Maunse nkae naijan, puah klus luman	Malus tahan iha rai, bua ne'e mamuk	*Manus* leaves on the ground, *puah* is empty
Ho mit man	Ó bele haree rasik	See for yourself
Nukat ko Bi	(labele komprende)	(unintelligible)
Hi luan-luan	Ó nia fatin sira ne'e - restu la rona	Your places, - the rest unintelligible
Mimaof puah-manus	Defende bua-malus	Guard the *puah manus*[16]
Mimaof uki tefu	Defende hudi no masin midar	Guard the bananas and the sugar

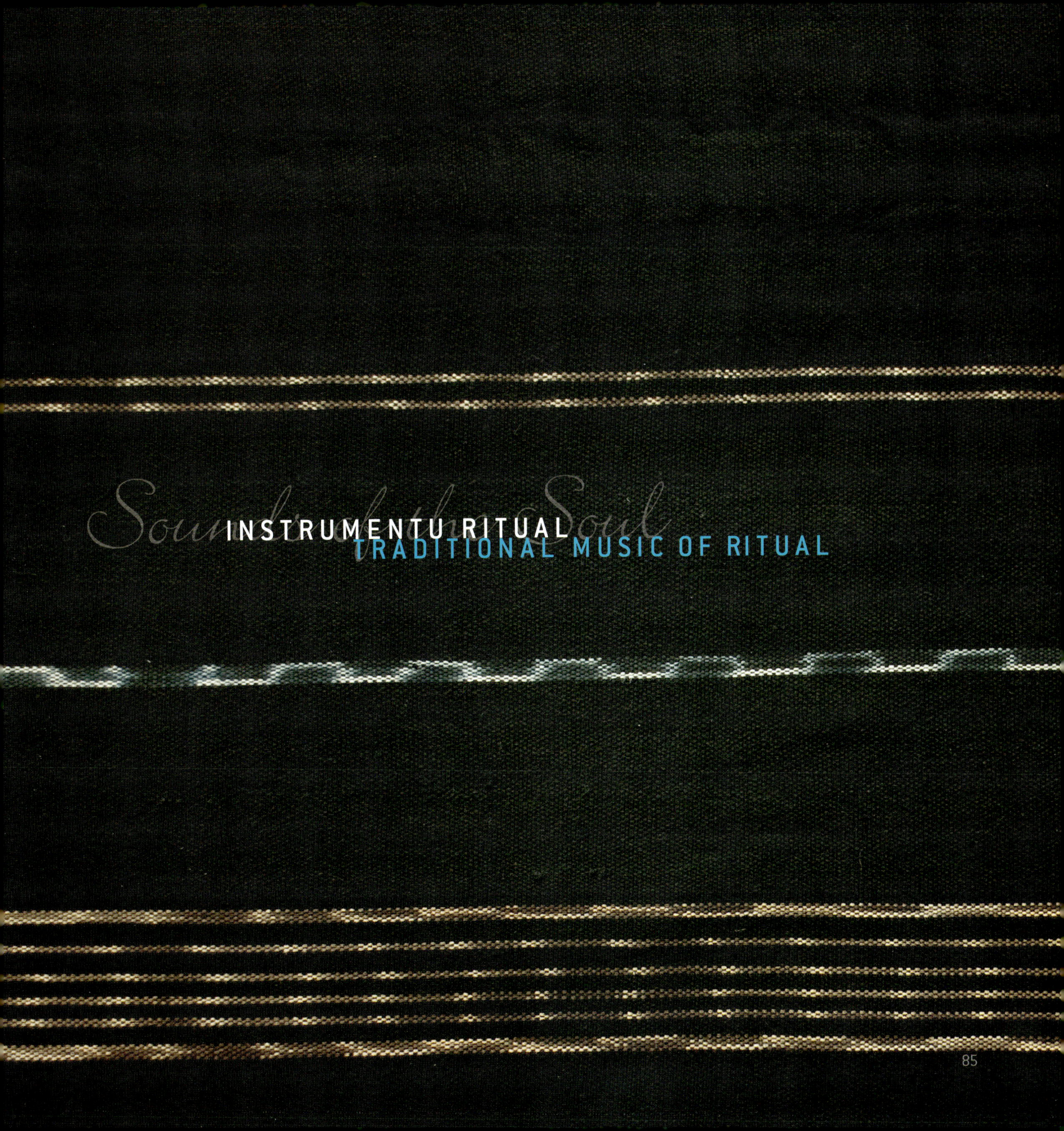

Sounds of the Soil

INSTRUMENTU RITUAL

TRADITIONAL MUSIC OF RITUAL

INTRODUCTION

Timorese culture is steeped in ritual and *lulik*. *Lulik* is a Tetun word, meaning forbidden, holy or sacred and is at the fundamental core of Timorese values. *Lulik* refers to the spiritual cosmos that contains the divine creator, the spirits of the ancestors, and the spiritual root of life including sacred rules and regulations that dictates relationships between people, and, people and nature.[17]

Much of the traditional music is closely connected with ritual and *lulik*. This is particularly evident in the most important events in village life, for example, the building of *uma luliks*, birth, death and marriage and the major events of the calendar year. Often specific music accompanies these ritual occasions. The music may only be instrumental, but more often will include song and dance. Traditional music also plays a central role in all agricultural festivals. Particular dances such as *dahur odi*, a *tebedai* for the rice harvest, are performed for such events.

The ritual ceremonies for funereal occasions are an important part of Timorese life. The Timorese believe that long after people are dead they can influence the living and the dead are treated with honour and reverence.[18] Ceremonies for the dead may reoccur at periodic intervals for years after a person has died, music will usually accompany these celebrations. Some musical instruments are designated to be played only for ritual occasions, such as the *titir* drum from the Lautein district. After it is played it is stored in its rightful place inside the *uma lulik*.[19] Other instruments such as the *baba dook* and *tala* are multifunctional, being played both for ritual ceremonies and in more lighthearted celebrations. Sometimes the only instruments to accompany the singing for funereal occasions may be the mortars and pestles used for grinding the grain. Once a steady rhythm has been established, the mourners will sing songs as they grind the grain which will be part of feasting which takes place as part of the funeral. These songs usually have associations with the person who has died. Some songs are only sung in ceremonies for the dead, such as the Bunak song *Lolan* from the Bobonaru district and the Baikeno song Pankalalále from the Oekusi district.

Karau Dikur

Karau dikur ne'e instrumentu ida ne'ebé uza iha serimónia no atu fó hatene ka anúnsia buat ruma. *Karau dikur* hanesan instrumentu ida ne'ebé uza iha nasaun barak dezde uluk liu. Iha Timor, ema uza *karau dikur* atu fó sai anúnsiu bainhira ema boot ruma mai. Ema konsidera nia hanesan instrumentu simbóliku ida no lulik, tuir ema Timor nia fiar tradisionál. João Pedro ema Mambae ne'ebé hatene barak kona-ba kultura, no nia dehan, "Múzika buat fundamentál ida; ninia fatin mak iha rai-klaran. Ai nia sanak sira luan, maibé múzika hanesan ninia abut, no *karau dikur* hanesan ninia hun." *Tuir* istória, iha tempu uluk, *karau dikur* toka ba liurai sira. Jeralmente uza iha rai klaran.

Dala ruma karau ne'ebé ema hili ne'e oho iha fatin segredu maibé dala ruma mós oho iha ema barak nia oin; nune'e ema fiar katak iha buat ruma espesiál kona-ba dikur husi karau ida ne'e.

Ninia boot entre sentímetru 30 - 60, nakloke iha tutun ida no iha tutun seluk iha kuak ki'ik. Barak liu mak ema kose tiha ho mina hodi halo nia nabilan. Ninia maneira huu mak tau tutun ki'ik rabat ho ibun, no huu hanesan karik atu huu trombeta.

Nia prodús son diferente ba ema ida-idak. Porezemplu, karik iha son tolu ba Xefe Suku no son lima ka neen ba liurai-mane ka liurai-feto. Maibé nia mós bele uza, iha okaziaun ruma, ba ema baibain, no, nia mós uza hodi anúnsia tempu udan.

> EZEMPLU AUDIO *karau dikur* CD TRACK/FAIXA 5
> EZEMPLU AUDIOVIZUÁL DVD SENA 1-6

Kokotere

Kokotere (pokotere - Naueti) instrumentu ida husi au no tali tahan, hanesan trombeta, ne'ebé mai husi foho iha distritu Baukau, Lautein, no Vikeke. Nia sempre uza mesak; la akompaña ho instrumentu seluk. Ninia funsaun mak atu simu bainaka ka anúnsia buat ruma, nu'udar tradisaun ne'ebé tun mai husi bei'ala sira.

Tubu au ne'e maizumenus metru ida ho balu naruk no ninia luan mak sentímetru 5. Ninia tutun mak tali tahan falun tiha halo forma kabuar, ne'ebé hatutan ba tubu sentrál ho tamañu ne'ebé hanesan. Depois, iha tan fatin tau ba ibun (iha lian Inglés ema bolu mouthpiece) ne'ebé forma kuadradu ne'ebé sentímetru 12 x 14 x 0.5. 'Nanál' ki'ik ida (bele husi au ka *karau dikur*) mak hatama iha ne'ebá, ho ninia tutun mós rabat malu ho kuak ne'ebé ibun kona ba. 'Nanál' ne'e kaer metin iha ninia fatin ho tali ka fita.

Kokotere famozu iha tempu Portugés no Indonézia nian, maibé ami só hetan múziku na'in rua, husi Wai-ole (besik Venilale.) Ema ne'ebé hatene toka *kokotere* kuaze la iha ona, entaun kuandu iha eventu ruma ka festa ruma iha Baukau ne'ebé presiza *kokotere*, sira tenke mai husi Venilale.

Ton rua ne'ebé ami grava tiha husi *kokotere* mak F no Ab iha 'C klaran' nia okos. Tokadór kaer *kokotere* orizontalmente ho liman rua, ho 'ibun fatin' iha liman rua nia klaran, no huu, no mós halo lian husi ninia kakorok dala ida. Ida ne'e halo 'nanál' nakdoko no amplifika son atu tun liu tubu. Depois, tokadór xupa fali nanál ho movimentu ne'ebé la para, atu lian kontinua nafatin. Dala ruma akontese asidente bainhira múziku ida xupa fali nanál ki'ik ne'e sai husi ibun fatin, tama ninia kakorok, no nisik nia besik mate.

Parte kabuar la aguenta kleur. Hafoin toka, múziku normalmente soe tiha parte kabuar ne'e, no dala ruma instrumentu tomak nia soe de'it. Tubu au mós labele uza ba tempu naruk. Susar mós atu hetan tubu au ho ninia naruk metru 1.5 ne'ebé loos, la'os kleuk. Nune'e, *kokotere* ne'e instrumentu ida ne'ebe raro duni, no iha perigu nia laran atu lakon.

90

Karau Dikur

The *karau dikur* is an instrument associated with ceremony and announcement. It is essentially the Timorese version of a cow horn, an instrument which has been employed in many countries of the world for centuries. In Timor it is used, for example, to announce the arrival of someone important, like the president. It is revered as a sacred and symbolic instrument, bound up in the traditional beliefs of the East Timorese. A custodian of Mambae culture, Joäo Pedro eloquently expressed the importance of the *karau dikur*: "Music is in the middle of the land, fundamental, the branches of the trees are wide, but music is the root, the buffalo horn is like the trunk of the tree."[20] Legend has it that in the times of the ancestors, the *karau dikur* was played for kings and queens.[21] It is generally played in the central mountain regions of Timor.

The *karau dikur* is made of buffalo horn. Sometimes, the buffalo used for the *karau dikur* is killed in secret and other times, in front of many people. In the latter case, the Timorese believe there is something special about the horn made from this buffalo.

The *karau dikur* varies in size from 30 cm to 60 cm, and is open at one end with a small hole at the other. Many of them are polished or oiled, making the surface very shiny. It is played by placing the small end in the corner of the mouth and pursing the lips to blow as would be done to play a bugle or trumpet.

Different sounds are produced on it for different people. For example, there might be three sounds for the *xefe suku*, the chief of the village, and five or six sounds for the king or queen. However, it can, on occasion, be used for ordinary people as well and is often used to herald the monsoonal rains in the wet season.

Kokotere *keko or koke in Fataluku*

The *kokotere (pokotere -Naueti)* is a trumpet-like instrument made of bamboo and palm leaf that comes originally from the central mountainous regions of the districts to the east of East Timor (Baukau, Lautein and Vikeke). It is an exclusively solo instrument used on ceremonial occasions as an instrument of announcement or welcome or at parties, part of an oral tradition passed down from the ancestors.

The bamboo tube is about 1.5 m long and approximately 5 cm in diameter. The palm bell is fastened to a bamboo tube extension that must match the bore of the existing bamboo tube. The mouthpiece has a rectangle of 12 to 14 cm x 0.5 cm cut out of the bamboo, into which is inserted a 'tongue' or reed made out of bamboo or buffalo horn that is flush with the hole and held in place by twine or tape (see previous page).

While the *kokotere* was prevalent in Portuguese and Indonesian times, our search for performers revealed only two musicians from Wai-ole, a village to the east of Venilale, and there was talk of a musician in a remote village near Kelikai on Mt Matebian. For any important functions or parties in Baukau the players come from Venilale district to play this instrument, as hardly anyone plays *kokotere* anymore.

The two pitches on the *kokotere* recorded are F and Ab below middle C. The player holds the *kokotere* horizontally with both hands, one each side of the mouthpiece, and blows into it while pushing the palm 'tongue' down and vocalising with his vocal chords. This vibrates the palm tongue and amplifies the sound down the tube/bell. The player then sucks the palm tongue up in a continuous motion, to keep the sound going. There have been some accidents in this process where musicians sucked the tongue right out of the mouthpiece and almost choked!

The palm bell does not last very long. After playing it the musician tends to throw away the bell (and sometimes the whole instrument) thus the *kokotere* is essentially a disposable instrument. The bamboo tube making up the rest of the instrument also does not last very long, but finding completely straight bamboo lengths of 1.5 m is not easy. As a result the *kokotere* is a rare instrument in danger of extinction.

AUDIO EXAMPLE of the *kokotere* **CD TRACK 7**
AUDIO VISUAL EXAMPLE **DVD SCENES 7-12**

Tohin

Tohin ne'e tambór silindru boot ida ho ulun ida ne'ebé normalmente ema hatuur iha rai. Nia mós bele kesi rabat ho lutu ida ka tau iha tara bandu ida nia sorin. *Tohin* signifika 'baku maka'as.'

Tohin instrumentu lulik ida, no ema fiar katak nia iha espíritu ida iha laran. *Tohin* pertense ba uma-lulik no uza ba serimónia no tempu espesiál. Karau nia raan sei uza bainhira ema halo *tohin*, ne'e karik hanesan batizmu ne'ebé ema fó ba tohin. Ida ne'e hanesan parte misteriozu no segredu ne'ebé haleu *tohin*.

Atu halo *tohin* ema uza ai ne'ebé moris iha foho Timor-Leste nian; karik tamba ne'e mak ita hetan tohin iha knua sira iha distritu Manufahi, Emera, Ainaro, Likisá. Ema mane mak dere *tohin*. Tokadór sira uza ai-tanutuk boot rua no tenke dere maka'as duni. Ema kole lailais, entaun múziku sira dere troka malu, no bele dere durante oras barak nia laran. Tohin-ulun halo husi karau nia kulit ne'ebé ema dada no estika tiha. Hodi hametin karau-kulit ne'e ema prega ho pregu ai. *Tohin* nia tamañu baibain mak maizumenus diámetru sentímetru 40 no 35 aas. Ai-tanutuk nia tamañu mak sentímetru 35 x 5.

> **EZEMPLU AUDIO** of the *tohin* **CD TRACK/FAIXA 15**
> **EZEMPLU AUDIOVIZUÁL** **DVD SENA 13-18**

ISTÓRIA LULIK IDA SOBRE KRIASAUN TOHIN

Uluk bainhira bei'ala sira halo serimónia, sira la iha instrumentu ruma atu uza hodi akompaña sira-nia knananuk. Loron ida, sira oho karau ida no deside atu uza ninia kulit nu'udar tambór nia kulit, maibé sira tenke habai maran karau-kulit ne'e. Depois sira ko'a ai-hun boot espesiál ida no ko'a sai tiha ninia klaran, no estika karau nia kulit hodi taka kuak iha rohan ida. Tuir istória, tohin mai husi Ainaru no Ramelau.

The *tara bandu* is an altar, " a round, tiered structure built of stone and earth. A circular wall of 'interlaced rocks" encloses a flattened mound of piled earth. The centre of the altar itself is marked by a high cairn of rocks. At the centre of the cairn, stands the altar post shrine, the *ai-tosa,* a tree trunk approximately five feet in height. The post branches out into three prongs, described as 'teeth' in ritual language. Flat offering stones called 'placing stones' surround the base of the post. The *tohin* sits on the southeastern edge of the cairn." [22]

Tihak

Iha oras madrugada, ita bele rona knananuk peskadór Ataúru nian bainhira sira sai ba soe rede. Sira kanta ho ritmu ida ne'ebé hanesan ho ritmu husi laloran ne'ebé baku kona bero nia sorin. Jeralmente knananuk tradisionál Ataúru nian kanta lahó instrumentu ne'ebé akompaña, no dala barak sira kanta bainhira dansa *dahur*. Instrumentu múzika sira iha Ataúru uitoan de'it, no *tihak* (*baba dook boot*) hanesan instrumentu úniku ida ne'ebé só hetan de'it iha Ataúru. Nia mai husi Makili. Só mane sira mak dere nia. Ema konsidera *tihak* nu'udar instrumentu lulik ida.

Bainhira la uza *tihak,* ninia na'in sei hasubar *tihak* iha ninia uma laran. Nia iha ulun ida de'it, halo husi bibi nia kulit. Nia forma atu hanesan ho *baba dook* maibé nia boot liu fali: naruk entre sentímetru 90-100 no luan entre sentímetru 25-30.

Tokadór tuur iha rai, ho hatoba *tihak* iha ninia ain leten. Nia toka ritmu simplis ne'ebé repete de'it, no kanta dala ida. Maizumenus ninia nota mak Ab.

EZEMPLU AUDIO *tihak* CD TRACK/FAIXA 17
EZEMPLU AUDIOVIZUÁL DVD SENA 13-18

ISTÓRIA LULIK IDA KONA-BA KRIASAUN TIHAK

Uluk, bei'ala sira la iha buat ida atu uza hodi akompaña sira-nia kanta. Ne'e mak sira sa'e ba foho Makadade no husu espíritu sira atu fó instrumentu ida ba sira atu uza bainhira kanta. Espíritu sira fó hatene ba ema sira ne'e oinsá mak bele halo tihak. Ema Ataúru hare'e tihak hanesan instrumentu múzika lulik ida.

Titir

Tambór tipu espesiál ida ho naran *titir* mai husi Iliomar no Luro, iha distritu Lautein. Artista bahat ai no halo figura hanesan ema. Iha versaun mane no versaun feto. Versaun mane lori naran *titir nami* no versaun feto iha naran *titir tufur*. Família boot ida-idak sempre iha *titir* ida, feto ka mane nian. Bainhira la uza ba toka, entaun *titir* tenke rai iha uma-lulik. Tambór rua ne'e iha papel boot iha povu nia moris, no ema só toka sira ba objetivu espesífiku ruma. Razaun boot mak bele uza nia mak atu fó hatene bainhira buat ida amiasa knua tomak. Knua ida-idak iha estilu diferente ba *titir nami* no *titir tufur*, konforme balada ne'ebé sira fiar ba. Porezemplu, ba família ne'ebé fiar katak sira-nia bei'ala sira mai husi lafaek, entaun sira reza ba lafaek no fiar katak nia sei hanetik sira, no sira halo sira-nia *titir* ho figura lafaek nian.

Sira fiar katak sira-nia bei'ala sira mai husi lekirauk karik, entaun sira fiar ba nia no bahat sira-nia *titir* tuir nia. Hanesan ho samea, no seluk tan. Figura báziku ba *titir* mak ema nia isin lahó ulun.

Durante okupasaun Indonézia, *titir nami* no *titir tufur* sunu hamutuk ho uma-lulik. Só foin lailais ne'e mak tambór sira ne'e no lisan relasiona ho sira hahú moris filafali.

Múziku, antropólogu, no hakerek na'in Margaret King visita Timor iha 1963, no nia haree *titir*, no iha tempu ne'ebá *titir* ladún barak ona. Nia hakerek hanesan ne'e:

95

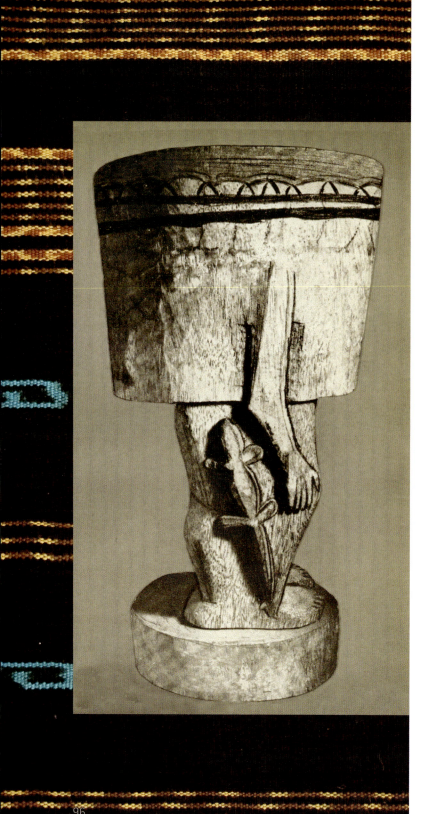

"Ko'a tiha husi ai-tali nia hun, ninia ain sira kuadradu no boot no hamriik metin iha ninia fundasaun nia leten, iha suku laran, parese katak nia hatene an katak nia importante. Liman ki'ik rua tun husi ninia sorin, liman fuan besik lafaek lulik ne'ebé dolar sa'e husi ain sira. Iha mós lasan no husar simplis. Ninia parsera tambór feminina ki'ik kompara ho mane ne'e, no nia lori lafaek ne'e iha kabun."

Bobakasa/Tambór

Bobakasa ne'e tambór ho ulun rua, ne'ebé bele ki'ik ka natoon. Ninia luan mak maizumenus sentímetru 35. Kulit normalmente husi bibi nia kulit. Tokadór hamriik no baku sorin ida ho ai-tanutuk rua. Liman ida, normalmente liman karuk, ho tan tali mahar ida ne'ebé tara husi kakorok, mak suporta *bobakasa* ne'e. Ai-tanutuk ne'ebé uza hodi dere nia mak bolu *bobakasa girte* iha dalen Makasae. Ai-tanutuk sira ne'e mihis tebes ho tutun kabuar.

Bobakasa konsidera instrumentu lulik ida no ema hotu respeita nia. Timoroan bele halo juramentu ba bandera nasionál, ne'ebé hetan respeitu boot iha Timor-Leste nia laran, ka bele halo juramentu iha nome de *bobakasa*.

EZEMPLU AUDIO *bobakasa* CD TRACK/FAIXA 16
EZEMPLU AUDIOVIZUÁL DVD SENA 13-18

Popokasa

Popokasa mós tambór ida husi Iliomar no Luro. Nia hamriik iha rai, iha ain haat no forma silindru, atu hanesan ho ke'e ne'ebé Oekusi nian. Populasaun lokál konsidera hanesan instrumentu lulik ida, só uza durante tempu selebrasaun hanesan festa kazamentu ba ema boot importante nian, ka bainhira hakoi ema mate.

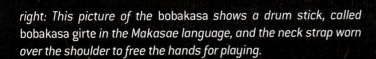

above: This titir *is the modern version of the* titir *described by Margaret King in 1963 (left). The* titir nami *and* titir tufur *are still made but the features on them are painted rather than carved and it is kept in a secret place away from general viewing.*

right: This picture of the bobakasa *shows a drum stick, called* bobakasa girte *in the Makasae language, and the neck strap worn over the shoulder to free the hands for playing.*

Tohin

The *tohin* is a large, cylindrical, single-headed drum that mostly sits on the ground. It can also be tied to a fence or placed beside a *tara bandu*. The *tara bandu* is generally placed in front of the *uma lulik*. *Tohin* means *baku maka'as*, to play loud or play hard.

The *tohin* is a sacred instrument, as it is believed to contain a spirit. The *tohin* belongs to the traditional house and is for special, ceremonial use. The blood from a buffalo is used in the making of the *tohin*, as if to baptize it. This is part of the secrecy and mystery surrounding the *tohin*.[23]

The wood for making the *tohin* comes from the mountains in East Timor, which is perhaps why it is most often found in the mountain villages of districts such as Manufahi, Emera, Ainaro and Likisá. It varies in size, with an average size of approximately 40 cm in diameter by 35 cm in length and the beaters often measuring about 5 cm x 35 cm.

The *tohin* is played by men. The player uses two large wooden beaters and strikes the drum with considerable force. As it is exhausting to play, the musicians beat the *tohin* in relay, often playing it for hours. The skin of the *tohin* is buffalo, stretched over the head of the drum and nailed into place by large wooden nails. Sometimes the skin is glued or braced to the drum.

AUDIO EXAMPLE of the *tohin* CD TRACK 15
AUDIO VISUAL EXAMPLE DVD SCENES 13-18

A LULIK STORY ABOUT THE CREATION OF THE TOHIN

Myth has it that the tohin originated from Ainaro and Ramelau. When the ancestors performed their ritual ceremony, they didn't have instruments to accompany their singing. They killed a buffalo and decided to use the skin for a drum. Firstly they dried it and then they carved out a large hollow piece of wood from a special tree and stretched the skin over the hole at one end.[24]

Tihak

In the pre-dawn hours you can often hear the song of the fishermen of Ataúru float across the water as they go out in their boats for the day's fishing. The rhythm of their song almost seems to keep time with the gentle rocking of the sea against the boat. The singing of traditional songs on Ataúru is generally unaccompanied, and most often sung when people dance the *dahur*.

There are only a few instruments on Ataúru and the *tihak*, (a large *baba dook boot*) unique to the island, is one of them and comes from one of the villages on the island, Makili.

Only men play the *tihak*, and they are known locally as the drummers of Makili. The *tihak* is regarded as a *lulik* instrument. When it is not played it is hidden away in the drummer's house.

The *tihak* is a large single-headed drum made of wood. Goat skin is stretched over the drum-head. It is similar in shape to the *baba dook*, but much larger. The *tihak* is about 90 to 100 cm in length with a diameter of about 25 to 30 cm.

The player usually sits cross-legged on the ground with the *tihak* lying over his legs, and plays a slow repetitive beat whilst singing. The pitch of the *tihak* is approximately Ab.

AUDIO EXAMPLE of the *tihak* **CD TRACK 17**
AUDIO VISUAL EXAMPLE **DVD SCENES 13-18**

A LULIK STORY ABOUT THE CREATION OF THE TIHAK

The story told, is that the ancestors had nothing to accompany their singing, so they climbed to the top of Mt Makadade and asked the spirits for an instrument to accompany their song. The spirits presented them with instructions on how to make the tihak. The people of Ataúru regard this drum as sacred.

above right: Ameta Jorge Ximenes Mendonca heating the bobakasa drum skin to tighten it, thereby improving the sound

below right: Goat drum skin of the bobakasa

left: Ameta Jorge Ximenes Mendonca playing the bobakasa

Titir

A special type of drum called the *titir* is regarded as *lulik* and comes from Iliomar and Luro in the Lautein district. The basic design for all the *titir* is the human body without a head (see page 96).

It is carved in the shape of a human figure and there is a male and a female version of the drum. The male drum is called *titir nami*, and the female drum is *titir tufur*. Each family clan either has a female or a male drum. When *titir nami* and *titir tufur* are not being played they are kept in their proper place, the *uma lulik*. Both *titir nami* and *titir tufur* play a significant role in the lives of the people of the village and are only played for specific purposes.

The main purpose of *titir nami* and *titir tufur* is to sound the alarm, calling people to attention in matters that will affect the entire clan. Different *knuas* (hamlets) have different designs for *titir nami* and *titir tufur*, depending on their specific animal belief. For example, if the family believes that their ancestors came from the crocodile, then they worship the crocodile and believe that it will be the protector of the family, so a crocodile is carved on the *titir*. If the family believes their ancestors came from monkey then they worship the monkey, so the monkey will be carved on the *titir*. The same goes for the snake, and so on.[25]

During Indonesian occupation *titir nami* and *titir tufur* were burned along with the *uma luliks* (they were always kept inside the *uma luliks*). Only very recently has there been a revival of these drums and the customs associated with them.

The musician, anthropologist and writer Margaret King visited Timor in 1963, she described the *titir* she was shown, which even then was very rare: "Carved from the butt of a large palm, the huge squared feet, with toes pointing slightly inwards, were planted firmly on the plinth as it stood in the *suko*, supremely aware of its own importance. Small arms extended from the sides, fingertips level at one point with the sacred crocodile which crawled up the bulging legs towards the lower trunk of the body: a rudimentary marking of penis and navel decorated the front of this male drum while its female counterpart, smaller in every way, carried the crocodile carving in the abdomen." [26]

Bobakasa/Tambór

The *bobakasa* is a double-headed drum, which can be a small or medium sized. The one in the picture at left, has a diameter of about 35cm. The drum skin is usually goat. The player stands to play and beats one side of the drum with both drum sticks, holding it in place with a neck strap while balancing it with one hand - usually the left. The drum sticks are called *bobakasa girte* in the Makasae language, and are thin wooden sticks with knobbed ends.

The *bobakasa* is regarded as a sacred instrument and highly respected by the people. The Timorese can swear oaths to the flag, which is deeply honoured in Timor - or they can swear oaths in the name of the *bobakasa*.[27]

AUDIO EXAMPLE of the *bobakasa* **CD TRACK 16**
AUDIO VISUAL EXAMPLE **DVD SCENES 13-18**

Popokasa

The *popokasa* is a drum from Iliomar and Luro. It stands on the ground and is a cylindrical drum similar to the *ke'e* (four-legged standing drum) from Oekusi.

This drum is also regarded as *lulik* and played at times of celebration, such as the marriage of an important person or funerals.

INSTRUMENTU SIRA IHA MORIS LOROLORON
INSTRUMENTS OF DAILY LIFE

Uluk liu se karik ita la'o iha to'os ka natar laran iha distritu lorosa'e nian, hanesan Baukau no Lautein, dala ruma ita bele rona lian fuik ruma ne'ebé mai derrepente de'it, no husu ba ita-nia an, "saida mak ne'e?" Bele ema mak toka *fiku* ka *pai koe-koe* ka *kakalo*, ka dala ruma son ne'ebé ho melodia kapás ne'ebé mai husi *kakal'uta*. Instrumentu sira ne'e nia funsaun prinsipál mak atu hata'uk balada sira no manu sira ne'ebé bele estraga natar ka to'os. Ohin loron raru atu rona instrumentu sira ne'e, maibé dala ruma ita sei rona ema hatudu iha festivál ruma.

In the past, if you walked through rice or corn fields in the districts to the east of Timor such as Baukau or Lautein, you might have heard a harsh sound come from nowhere and wondered what it was. It could have been someone playing the *fiku* or *pai koe-koe*, or the *kakalo*, or a more melodious and mellow sound might have been heard from the *kakal'uta*. The main purpose of these instruments was to scare animals and birds from eating the crops. These days it is rare to hear these instruments, apart from the odd appearance in festivals.

Kakal'uta

Kakal'uta halo husi ai-pokura ne'ebé moris iha ai-laran Lautein nian. Nia iha ton oioin. Ema ne'ebé hela besik to'os no tau matan ba to'os mak toka *kakal'uta*, tamba sira tenke hamahan to'os ne'e no *kakal'uta* nia lian bele hata'uk lekirauk no manu-kakatua sira. Uluk bainhira ema sei uza iha to'os, sira tara au-tubu silindru sira ne'e. Ohin loron ita rona dala ruma de'it iha festivál.

Bainhira ema uza nia ohin loron, iha tubu au silindru pár rua: tolu ne'ebé tara hamutuk ba ema ida, no tolu tan ba ema ida tan. Au ne'e naruk kuaze sentímetru 100 no luan mak 12. Sira tara ho tali husi ai ida ne'ebé suporta husi riin ki'ik rua. Pár naktarak ne'e toka husi ema na'in rua maibé ho ritmu repetitivu ida de'it. Sira dere lailais ho ai-tanutuk rua. Maizumenus *kakal'uta* nia ton iha gravasaun mak G#, B, no C.

Múzika ne'ebé kria husi *kakal'uta* atu hanesan marimba, mak xilofone husi Áfrika ne'ebé mosu tinan atus tolu liubá. Liafuan marimba mai husi dalen Kimbundu iha Angola, ne'ebé mós sofre nu'udar kolónia Portugál nian.

Soldadu Áfrika balu serbisu iha Lautein tinan atus ida liubá, mak nune'e karik ita hanoin dala ruma *kakal'uta* mosu iha Timor-Leste iha tempu ne'ebá.

EZEMPLU AUDIO *kakal'uta* CD TRACK/FAIXA 18
EZEMPLU AUDIOVIZUÁL DVD SENA 19-21

Kakalo

Kakalo (*bobakasa-au*, Naueti) mak *tambór* au naksakat ida. Au nia sorin ida mak halo kabeer ho katana, mak halo sakat iha ne'ebá iha seksaun tomak nia naruk. Ninia kaer fatin mós husi au ne'e. Tokadór tuku *kakalo* nia sorin ho au ki'ik ida. Ninia son diferente konforme tuku iha ne'ebé. Uluk uza *kakalo* hodi duni sai fahi sira husi to'os laran.

Kakalo halo iha Lospalos iha fulan Janeiru tinan 2011 husi múziku Australianu ida naran Tony Hicks ho ajuda husi Señor Mario da Costa.

Fiku Ka Pai Koe-Koe

Fiku, mós bolu ho naran *pai koe-koe*, hanesan instrumentu ki'ik ida ne'ebé huu mak halo lian. Ninia naruk mak entre sentímetru 25-50, iha forma kuhus-meik no halo husi au tahan.

Atu huu nia, tokadór tenke hatama nanál ba iha ibun fatin nia laran no huu maka'as! Bele halo liu tiha ton ida de'it, se karik tokadór tau liman fuan ida ka rua iha kuhus nia okos. Son ne'ebé prodús bele hata'uk manu ida ne'ebé fuik liu!

Pai signifika fahi iha dalen Fataluku, no ita bele fiar katak la iha fahi ida ne'ebé sei kontinua buka hahan iha to'os laran bainhira nia rona *pai koe-koe* nia lian siak ne'e.

Kakalo

The *kakalo* (*bobakasa-au*, Naueti) is a bamboo slit drum. One side of the bamboo is cut flat with a machete, and then a slit is cut into the centre of the flat side, right down the length of the bamboo from node to node. Part of the next segment of bamboo is kept so that a handle can be carved. The player strikes the side of the *kakalo* with a small bamboo beater. It is capable of different sounds depending on where it is hit. The *kakalo* was used in the past for scaring pigs from eating the crops.

The *kakalos* shown here were made in workshops in Lospalos in January 2011, by Australian musician, Tony Hicks, under the instruction of Señor Mario da Costa.

Fiku or Pai koe-koe

The *fiku* or *pai koe-koe* is a small palm trumpet, it can be various lengths from 25 cm to 50 cm and made from tightly wound bamboo leaves shaped into a cone (see page 107). To play it, the player must purse their lips, insert their tongue into the mouthpiece and blow hard! More than one pitch is possible if the player inserts a finger or fingers into the bottom of the cone. The sound produced would scare away the most foolhardy bird!

Pai means pig in Fataluku the language of Lautein, and one suspects that no self-respecting pig would have stayed hunting for food amongst crops too long when they heard the sound of the *pai koe-koe*! [28]

Kakal'uta

The *kakal'uta* is a log xylophone made from the wood of the *pokura* tree and found in the jungle of the Lautein District. The *kakal'uta* was played by the people who lived in the fields, one of their jobs was to protect the crops. They played the *kakal'uta* to scare away monkeys and cockatoos from eating the crops. In the past when the *kakal'uta* was played in the fields, one set of suspended cylindrical tubes would be used. Now rarely heard, it is occasionally played in festivals.

In its contemporary use there is a pair of suspended pitched cylindrical tubes, played by two people. Each set in the pair consists of 3 tubes, approximately 12 cm in diameter by 100 cm in length suspended with rope from a cross beam, which may be fixed to a tall freestanding frame. The suspended pairs are played with unison rhythm, by two musicians using two wooden beaters and beating a fast and repetitive rhythm. The pitches of the *kakal'uta* on the recording are approximately G#, B, and C.

The music created by the *kakal'uta* is similar in sound and rhythm to the marimba, the deep-toned xylophone that originated in Africa around the early eighteenth century. The word marimba comes from Kimbundu dialect, one of the Bantu languages in Angola, a country also colonized by the Portuguese. Soldiers from Africa were stationed in Lautein District in the early 1900s, so perhaps the *kakal'uta* evolved in East Timor during this time.

AUDIO EXAMPLE of the *kakal'uta* **TRACKS 18 CD**
AUDIO VISUAL EXAMPLE DVD SCENES 19-21

Kafu'i

Bainhira ita la'o lemo-rai iha Timor-Leste, se karik ita-nia matan haree didiak, ita bele haree *kafu'i* iha to'os na'in nia bolsu ka kesi hamutuk ho ninia katana. Nia uza hodi bolu karau, atu bolu manu fuik, ka atu hata'uk manu sira ne'ebé atu estraga to'os ka natar. Nia mós bele toka *kafu'i* bainhira deskansa husi serbisu. *Kafu'i* bele hetan iha distritu hotu iha Timor-Leste nia laran.

Jeralmente *kafu'i* toka mesak, no melodia sira hatutan mai husi avón sira. Bele halo husi au ka ai, ho tamañu no naruk ne'ebé entre 18 to'o 80 cm. Dala ruma *kafu'i* husi ai ema ko'a tiha ho deseñu ida.

Ba instrumentu sira ne'ebé iha kuak-liman liu tiha rua, melodia sira jeralmente livre, triste, no ritmu sira naran de'it. Bainhira ema husu ba tokadór, "Saida mak múzika ne'e?" nia bele responde karik, "Ida ne'e ha'u aprende husi hau-nia apá sira, no bainhira ha'u toka ne'e, ha'u hanoin ba tempu uluk no ema sira ne'ebé lakon iha tempu ne'ebá."

Kafu'i husi ai mai husi foho iha parte Oekusi, Kovalima, no Bobonaru no haree hanesan ho *feku* ka flauta ne'ebé hetan iha foho iha Timor-Osidentál ne'ebá. Iha similaridade ne'ebé hanesan iha fatin hotu kona-ba oinsá atu uza instrumentu ne'e.

Kafu'i iha modelu barak. Kuandu nia ki'ik, ninia ton aas. Sira ne'ebé la iha kuak-liman jeralmente husi ai, no tokadór kaer nia vertikalmente no huu ba ibun fatin. *Kafu'i* sira ne'e iha ton fundamentál ida, dala ruma 'sobreton' sira bele rona iha ton nia leten. Hatama liman fuan ida ba iha tutun kraik bele prodús ton seluk tan. *Kafu'i* ida ne'e rona hanesan manu nia lian, karik tanba ne'e mak ema uza nia hodi bolu manu fuik sira. Modelu balu mós kaer kalatan no huu hakat ibun fatin ne'ebé iha instrumentu nia klaran.

Kafu'i boot no *kafu'i ki'ik* ita bele hetan iha Likisá. Ida boot ne'e maizumenus sentímetru 80 x 2 ho notas husi Bb-Bb(Bb iha C klaran nia okos). Ninia kualidade ton ne'e kalma no oskuru. Ida ki'ik ho tamañu setímetru 65 x 1.5 no bele prodús notas entre A-A (hahú ho A ne'ebé iha C klaran nia leten). Kualidade ton iha variasaun ho notas aas mak 'nabilan' no notas okos mak oskuru. Instrumentu rua ne'e iha kuak haat no tokadór kaer nia vertikalmente no huu hakat ibun fatin.

Iha Ossu, *kafu'i* iha kuak-liman neen. Ai-pedasuk ki'ik ida, bobar ho tali, taka kuak iha ibun fatin iha flauta nia rohan, hodi halo *kafu'i* ne'e atu bele halimar ho notas aas no notas kraik hotu. Melodia sira ne'ebé komplexu bele halo ho *kafu'i* ida ne'e.

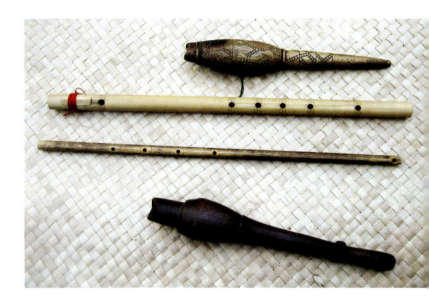

EZEMPLU AUDIO *kafu'i* CD TRACK/FAIXA 6
EZEMPLU AUDIOVIZUÁL DVD SENA 7-12

Lesun No Alu

Maski *lesun no alu* uza hodi fai batar ka foos, sira mós serve nu'udar instrumentu ba knaar na'in hodi akompaña sira-nia knananuk ka hananu. Kultura barak uza buat ne'e hotu nu'udar instrumentu. Iha Timor-Leste múzika hanesan ne'e iha tradisaun naruk liu no ita bele hetan iha fatin hotu iha rai laran.

Alu boot ne'e halo husi ai-sanak boot ida, ko'a tiha hodi halo knata mamuk ne'ebé iha kurva. Ai ne'ebé uza atu fai ka alu sira ne'e naruk metru rua. Knaar na'in hahú fai foos no kuandu estabelese ona ritmu no ton, ema ida mak kanta lidera knananuk ida, ne'ebé ajuda oras atu la'o lailais bainhira serbisu hela.

EZEMPLU AUDIO *lesun no alu* CD TRACK/FAIXA 11
EZEMPLU AUDIOVIZUÁL DVD SENA 7-12

Kafu'i

When travelling around East Timor, you might, if you are observant, see a *kafu'i* in the back pocket of a farmer, or tied onto his belt along with his machete. It is used to call the buffalo, to lure small birds or to scare birds away so they don't eat the crops. It is also played for pleasure during breaks from work. It is found throughout East Timor.

The *kafu'i* is generally used as a solo instrument and the tunes passed on by aural tradition. It is made of wood or bamboo, with sizes varying from 18 cm to 80 cm in length, the wooden *kafu'i* are occasionally decoratively carved.

On instruments with two or more finger holes, the tunes tend to be free-form melodies, often haunting and sad, the rhythms of these melodies are not specific. When asked, "what is the tune you play?" ... or "what do you play about", the player may respond, " it is a tune I learnt from my ancestors and when I play it, I am thinking about the past and all the people who were lost in the bad times."

The wooden *kafu'i* from the mountain regions of Oekusi, Kovalima and Bobonaru looks similar to the *feku* or flute found in the mountain regions of West Timor, and the use of the instrument in both cultures is similar too.

There are many different models of *kafu'i*. The smaller the *kafu'i*, the higher the pitch. The ones with no finger holes tend to be wooden, and held vertically, the player blows across the mouthpiece (shown right). These *kafu'i* have one fundamental pitch, sometimes overtones can be played above this pitch. Inserting a finger into the bottom end of the *kafu'i* can produce another pitch as well. This particular *kafu'i* sounds like a bird-call, which is perhaps why it is used in hunting to attract birds. Some models are held horizontally and blown across the mouthpiece that is placed in the middle of the instrument.

In Ossu, the *kafu'i* has six finger holes. A small piece of cane (shown below) is bound in place with string over a hole at the mouthpiece end of the *kafu'i* (a register hole) giving the instrument the ability

to play upper and lower octaves. Quite complex melodies can be played on this *kafu'i*.

The *kafu'i boot* (bass *kafu'i*) and *kafu'i ki'ik* (alto *kafu'i*) are found in Likisá. The *kafu'i boot* (see far right) is approximately 80 cm in length x 2 cm in diameter with a pitch range Bb - Bb (from the Bb just below middle C). The tone quality is dark and mellow. *Kafu'i ki'ik* (approximately 65 cm x 1.5 cm) has an octave range A - A (from the A above middle C). The tone quality is varied with the top notes sounding bright, while the low notes are darker. Both instruments have four holes and are held vertically to play, by blowing across the mouthpiece.

> AUDIO EXAMPLE of the *kafu'i* **CD TRACK 6**
> AUDIO VISUAL EXAMPLE **DVD SCENES 7-12**

Lesun no Alu

Although the mortar and pestle is a tool used to pound corn or rice, it doubles as a musical instrument for the workers to accompany their singing. Many cultures use the drone rhythms of mortar and pestles to accompany the singing of songs whilst working. In East Timor this kind of music-making is a very old tradition and is found throughout the country.

The large pestle is a wooden log, carved out to make a curved, hollow trough. The wooden poles (mortars) are about two meters tall. The workers begin pounding the grain and once a steady rhythmic drone is established a solo vocalist leads the singing of the song, which helps pass the time while working.

> AUDIO EXAMPLE of the *lesun no alu* **CD TRACK 11**
> AUDIO VISUAL EXAMPLE **DVD SCENES 7-12**

Rama

Rama ne'e rama-inan muzikál ne'ebé toka ho ibun, ne'ebé só hetan iha nusa Ataúru.

Uluk, Portugés sira uza Ataúru nu'udar fatin kastigu ba ema ne'ebé kontra sira-nia ukun, liuliu ema Timor no ema São Tomé e Príncipe no Angola. Ne'e la'os asidente katak *rama* ne'e hanesan ho instrumentu ida husi Angola ho naran - ŋ!ao. Instrumentu rua ne'e similar iha aspetu físiku no maneira ne'ebé uza atu toka nia, no ninia ton ne'ebé nia prodús. *Rama* nia naruk mak maizumenus sentímetru 60 cm no ai-mihis ne'ebé uza hodi dere nia mak naruk sentímetru 24 ho ninia luan mak 1/4.

Rama ne'e tau ba múziku nia ibun kraik. Liman ida tahan ninia tutun sorin, no liman ida kaer ai-mihis hodi dere ba talin. Tokadór muda ninia ibun uitoan, no mós aumenta ka hamenus ninia iis. Nune'e nia bele prodús 'sobreton' sira, bazeia husi ton fundamentál ne'ebé talin ne'e iha.

EZEMPLU AUDIO *rama* CD TRACK/FAIXA 2
EZEMPLU AUDIOVIZUÁL DVD SENA 1-6

Rama

The *rama* is a musical mouth bow found only on the remote island of Ataúru, to the north of Dili. It is played as an accompaniment to the *bidu* dance.

The Portuguese used Ataúru as a prison for colonial dissidents, mostly mainland Timorese and Africans from their colonies, in particular from São Tomé e Príncipe and Angola. It is no coincidence that the instrument which closely resembles the *rama* - the ŋ!ao - is a musical mouth bow played by the Bantu Bushmen from Angola. This similarity extends to the physical characteristics of both instruments, the way it is played and the pitches produced. The *rama* is approximately 60 cm in length. The bow is made of bamboo with a thin wire string attached to each end of the bamboo which keeps the bow curved and the wire string taut. The stick it is beaten with is about 24 cm long and 1/4 cm diameter, made from the wood of a coconut tree.

The *rama* is balanced against the musician's lower lip. One hand balances the opposite end of the bow, while the other strikes the bowstring with a small stick. By altering the mouth shape and changing the volume of air used, the player creates different overtones through the sympathetic vibration of air. The pitches are the series of harmonic intervals based on the fundamental string pitch.

AUDIO EXAMPLE of the *rama* CD TRACK 2
AUDIO VISUAL EXAMPLE DVD SECENES 1-6

Kakeit

Kakeit ne'e 'instrumentu ibun' ne'ebé bele hetan iha fatin hotu iha mundu rai klaran tomak, no kuaze tuan liu hotu. Versaun Timor-Leste nian atu hanesan versaun sira seluk ne'ebé ita hetan iha rejiaun Ásia Sudeste. Uluk, ema uza *kakeit* iha distritu hotu iha Timor-Leste nia laran, maibé ohin loron ita hetan iha Manufahi, Baukau, Oekusi, no Dili. Buat ne'e iha naran barak konforme ho dalen lokál. Iha Mambae - *snarko*; iha Baikeno - *knobe*; iha Waima - *rai rai*; iha Makasae - *nagu*; iha Fataluku - *pepuru*.

Kakeit bele halo husi au, besi, ka ai-tahan. Ninia naruk mak entre sentímetru 10 no 14, no nia iha nanál au ka besi. Ho ida au ne'e, tali ida kesi ba nanál ki'ik no dada ho tokadór nia liman fuan sira, no tokadór bele muda ninia ibun no aumenta ka hamenus ninia iis. Ida ne'e halo *kakeit* nia nanál nakdoko ka halo vibrasaun ho maneira oioin no prodús ton aas sira, bazeia husi ton fundamentál ida. Versaun besi iha ganxu ki'ik iha nanál nia rohan ne'ebé tokadór fekit, no halo ibun loke uitoan tan ka taka uitoan, muda ninia nanál rasik, no modifika ninia iis. Diferensa ne'ebé iha kona-ba ton entre *kakeit* sira depende ba materiá ne'ebé uza no mós ba abilidade tokadór nian.

Kakeit nia lian ki'ik no mamar, no ema gosta toka nia bainhira hein bibi ka karau. Iha Same, ema toka atu hata'uk kutun atu sira la han batar.

Dala ruma mós mane klosan sira toka *kakeit* hodi atrai feto raan sira. Iha istória ida Waima nian, konta husi katuas ida iha Triloka, besik Baukau: se mane klosan toka *rai rai* ba feto ne'ebé nia laran monu ba, iha feto ne'e nia janela okos, nune'e feto raan ne'e sei laran monu kedas ba nia. Tuir loos, feto raan ne'e toka *kafu'i* hodi hatán katak nia mós hakarak mane klosan ne'e.

EZEMPLU AUDIO *kakeit*	CD TRACK/FAIXA 3
EZEMPLU AUDIOVIZUÁL	DVD SENA 1-6

Tuir istória, oan kiak mane ida mak hamosu kakeit ba dahuluk. Iha loron ida nia huu halimar ho kaleen aat rua, koko hela atu halo múzika. Nia deside atu halo instrumentu ida atu nia sempre bele toka. Baihira nia remata halo ninia instrumentu ne'e, nia bá basar. Ema hakfodak no gosta ninia múzika, no husu nia kona-ba ninia múzika. Labarik ne'e hatán katak nia toka para ninia inan-aman nia klamar sira bele rona no hanoin nafatin atu tau matan ba nia. Ema barak gosta nia no ninia kakeit, no sira husu nia atu hanorin sira no halo kakeit barak tan. Durante tinan barak ona ema toka kakeit bainhira sira hakarak fó honra ba sira-nia bei'ala sira ka husu sira-nia bensa.

Bijol Meto

Se karik ita la'o iha tasi ibun ka estrada ninin ita bele hare'e labarik mane ida la'o halimar ho ninia maluk sira, toka hela viola ki'ik ida, halo ho liman de'it no halo iha uma, ho naran *bijol meto*. *Bijol meto* ne'e hetan barak liu iha Oekusi.

Bijol meto halo ho ai-pedasuk ida de'it. Nia talin haat halo husi tali keil ikan, dada tiha iha *bijol meto* nia 'ponte' ki'ik no bobar ba ai-habit ne'ebé iha instrumentu ne'e nia kakorok nia tutun.

Parese *bijol meto* ne'e eziste hahú kedas iha tempu Portugés. Parese mós hanesan versaun modifikadu husi ida naran braguinha, ne'ebé mak instrumentu ida ho tali lima ne'ebé mai husi Braga, Portugál. Buat ne'e mós konsege to'o Hawai'i durante migrasaun Portugés ba nusa sira ne'e iha sékulu 19. Iha ne'ebá mak ema komesa bolu nia ho naran ukelele ka 'asu-kutun haksoit:' uku signifika 'asu-kutun,' no lele signifika 'haksoit.'

EZEMPLU AUDIO *bijol meto* CD TRACK/FAIXA 10
EZEMPLU AUDIOVIZUÁL DVD SENA 13-18

Kakeit

The *kakeit* is a mouth instrument otherwise known as a Jaw harp or mouth harp that is found all over the globe, and is one of the oldest instruments in the world. The East Timorese version closely resembles some of those found in South East Asia. The *kakeit* was once played throughout Timor but it is now mostly confined to the Manufahi, Baukau, Oekusi and Dili districts. There are many names for the instrument, depending on the language group of the people. For example: Mambae - *snarko*, Baikeno - *knobe*, Waima - *rai rai*, Makasae - *nagu*, Fataluku - *pepuru*.

The *kakeit* is made of bamboo, coconut wood, metal or a leaf. It is around 10 cm to 14 cm in length and has a bamboo or metal tongue. With the bamboo model, a piece of string is tied to the end of the tongue and is pulled by the player's fingers, while simultaneously altering his mouth shape and the volume of air. This causes the bamboo tongue to vibrate in different ways and produce a series of overtones from a fundamental pitch. The metal version has a hook at the end of the tongue that the player flicks while making small adjustments with his mouth, tongue and airflow. The several differences seen in the pitch of instruments depends on the material used in construction and the ability of the player.

Myth has it that an orphan made the first kakeit. One day he was blowing through two bits of old tin trying to make music. He decided to make an instrument so he would always be able to play. When he finished making the kakeit he took it to the market place to play. People were so impressed they started asking him about his music. The boy said he played his instrument so that the spirit of his dead parents would remember to look after him. The people liked the boy and his kakeit and asked him to teach them and make more kakeits. Over the years people played the kakeit whenever they wanted to honour their ancestors or ask for their blessing.[29]

The sound of the *kakeit* is small and soft, often played for pleasure while minding the goats or buffalo. In Same, people play the *kakeit* (*snarko* - Mambae) to scare off the corn beetle so they won't eat the crops.

The *kakeit* is sometimes played by young men to attract young women. There is a Waima story told by an old man in Triloka, a village near Baukau, that if a young man plays the *rai rai* below the window of a girl he loves, she will fall in love with him. The girl in response is meant to play the *kafu'i*, indicating her desire to be wooed!

> **AUDIO EXAMPLE** of the *kakeit* **CD TRACK 3**
> **AUDIO VISUAL EXAMPLE** **DVD SCENES 1-6**

Bijol Meto

Walking along the side of the road or on a beach in East Timor a boy can sometimes be seen playing a hand-carved ukulele known as *bijol meto* as he strolls along singing with friends. The *bijol meto* (homemade ukulele) is found mostly in Oekusi.

The *bijol meto* is carved from a single piece of wood. It has four strings made of fishing line stretched over the bridge and fastened to the pegs, which are screwed into the back of the neck at the top of the instrument.

It is likely that the *bijol meto* has existed in East Timor since Portuguese times. It appears to be a modified version of the braguinha. This was a five-stringed instrument from Braga, Portugal, which made its way to Hawaii during the migration of Portuguese to the islands in the late nineteenth century. There it became known as the ukulele, or the 'jumping flea': uku in Hawaii means flea, and lele means to jump or leap.[30]

> **AUDIO EXAMPLE** of the *bijol meto* **CD TRACK 10**
> **AUDIO VISUAL EXAMPLE** **DVD SCENES 13-18**

Au

Instrumentu tipu flauta, ne'ebé hetan iha distritu Likisá. Nia kuaze hanesan duni ho ida naran pengbi, ne'ebé hetan iha Xina sudueste, no iha risku nia laran atu lakon husi mundu.

Ami deskobre *au* bainhira Tekee Media bá Likisá atu grava konjuntu muzikál ne'ebé toka múzika estilu dansa Portugeza nian.

Iha ne'ebá iha ema ida kaer *au*, ne'ebé iha lian mamar, no uza atu fó ton báziku ida ne'ebé sustenta nafatin, iha grupu tradisionál ne'ebé mós inklui *lakadou* no *kafu'i boot*. *Au* mós uza iha konjuntu la tradisionál.

Au halo husi *au* tubu rua ho tamañu diferente; ida ki'ik tama iha ida boot. Ida boot ne'e naruk maizumenus sentímetru 100 no luan 10, ho ida ki'ik ne'e naruk liután: sentímetru 110, maibé mihis fali: sentímetru 4. Ida mihis nia tutun rua nakloke hela, maibé ida luan ne'e nia tutun kraik taka naturalmente ho selat ne'ebé iha ona iha *au*. Tokadór huu ba ida ki'ik, no ida boot amplifika lian ne'e halo boot liután. Ton ne'ebé prodús husi tokadór huu hela 'sobreton,' mantein maizumenus nafatin. Só iha ton balu baixu nian (Bb, Eb, no A).

Au

The *au* (a bamboo wind instrument) found in the district of Likisá, has a remarkable resemblance to the *pengbi*, an endangered traditional musical instrument from Southwest China.[31]

We discovered the *au* when Tekee Media went to Likisá to record a Portuguese-style dance band. In one corner of the band was a musician with the *au*, which has a soft sound, and seems to be used as an accompanying drone in traditional ensembles made up of *lakadou*, *kafu'i boot* and *au* as well as in non-traditional ensembles like these Portuguese-style dance bands.

The *au* is a bamboo wind instrument, made up of two cylindrical tubes of different diameter and length, one fitting inside the other. The larger tube is approximately 100 cm x 10 cm in diameter, with the thinner, longer tube, approximately 120 cm x 4 cm in diameter, fitting inside the larger tube. Both ends of the slimmer (inner) bamboo tube are open, whereas the outer bamboo tube is closed at the bottom by the natural nodes of the bamboo. As the player blows into the inner tube the sound amplifies inside the tube encasing it. The pitch, achieved by the player blowing overtones, is fairly constant. There are only a few bass pitches (Bb, Eb and A).

122

N. PIRIS

Sounds of the Soul

KNANANUK TRADISIONÁL
TRADITIONAL SONG

Timor-Leste iha tradisaun riku tebes kona-ba hananu, no knananuk tuan barak loos. Knananuk tradisionál iha papel importante iha so-siadade ne'ebé tradisaun kulturál no muzikál pasa husi ibun ba ibun. Melodia la muda husi jerasaun ba jerasaun, maibé liafuan bele troka konforme situasaun. Liafuan iha tópiku ne'ebé uza ne'e livre, no bele konta kona-ba atividade lororon nian, konta istória, halo komiku, no mós bele kritika ba nai ulun sira.

Knananuk iha ba okaziaun barak no hola parte iha moris lororon nian. Iha mundu tomak no fatin hotu, knananuk sempre iha atu hakma'an kna'ar ne'ebé halo lororon. Knananuk iha ba kuda batar no ko'a hare. Knananuk ba karau sira mós iha. Bainhira mane sira tula sasán todan, knananuk ida bele ajuda sira. Peskadór sira kanta bainhira sira hean sira-nia bero, no sira mós kanta ba lenuk, ikan-lemur, no ba sipu molok foti sira atu halo dekorasaun ba uma tradisionál sira. Knananuk iha ba tempu fai batar, akompaña ho ritmu ne'ebé mai husi asaun fai ai ka fatuk. Ema kanta knananuk ba ai sira molok taa sira atu uza hodi halo uma.

Labarik sira kanta nu'udar parte ida iha sira-nia jogu sira. Ida hahú ho melodia no sira seluk tama no kanta to'o remata. Iha knananuk ba serimónia espesiál, porezemplu bainhira halo uma-lulik, ka bainhira atu kasa ikan-pari. Knananuk espesiál iha ba festivál agrikultura nian. Uluk, ema Timor kanta atu simu funu na'in sira bainhira fila mai husi funu.

Knananuk mate nian fó honra ba ema sira ne'ebé mate ona. Liafuan opsionál, no konta istória kona-ba Matebian ne'e, no istória husi ninia knua no família. Kanta ne'e la'o loron no kalan no la para até istória konta hotu. Importante katak kanta ne'e detallada: labele haluhan buat ida, ne'e para evita buat aat ida kona Matebian nia klamar ka ema sira ne'ebé sei moris hela iha knua laran. Kanta ne'e serve mós atu ajuda klamar ne'e atu 'la'o tuir dalan' hasoru ninia avón sira. Liafuan avón iha kontextu ne'e termu jerál ida.

Knananuk akompaña *dahur*. Knananuk nia ritmu fó ritmu di'ak ba dansarinu sira. Melodia normalmente diatonic (katak uza de'it notas husi klave espesífiku ida, porezemplu c maiór - C, D, E, F, G, A, B, C). Melodia balu la hanesan ne'e, porezemplu *bidu* tais mutin husi Suai, ne'ebé akompaña ho *raraun* no hananu. Iha *bidu* ida ne'e, kantadór kanta melodia ida ne'ebé bele haksoit bá-mai, uza vibrasaun lian no ornamentasaun, lian tun no sa'e derrepente no hakat notas (slides) no mós son ida ne'ebé hanesan fahi boot ida mak nakoron. Iha *dahur* baibain ida, melodia sei introdús tiha husi kantadór mesak ida, mane ka feto. Se mane karik, nia bele uza son alta. Partisipante sira sei responde hamutuk, hanesan koru, ba solo ne'e. Bele koru mane sira de'it, no koru feto de'it sei tuir, ka, koru bele inklui ema hotu.

NOTA Knananuk ida-idak nia dalen hakerek tuir ninia títulu. Dala barak koru ne'e uza armonia komplexu. Dala ruma mós sira kanta de'it melodia lahó armonia. Só melodia husi knananuk ida-ida mak hakerek iha livru ida ne'e. Knananuk tradisionál mak hili mak ladún koñe-sidu, no sira representa aspetu diferente husi kultura tradisionál. Knananuk sira iha livru ne'e hakerek iha dalen ne'ebé orijinál ba sira, ho tradusaun ba Tetun no Inglés. Knananuk sira bele rona iha CD laran. Knananuk sira hakerek ho sistema modernu no mós ho sistema número ne'ebé ema Timor barak hatene ona, ne'ebé introdús durante okupasaun Indonézia.

Timor has a rich tradition of singing and many traditional songs. Traditional songs play an important role in a society where cultural and musical traditions are passed on orally. Whilst the melody of songs are passed on generation to generation, the words change to suit the circumstances. Lyrics are topical and may recount the day's activities, tell a story, a joke, or even criticise the authorities.

Songs are sung for many occasions and are part of daily life. In cultures all over the world, songs are sung to help lighten the burden of daily physical work. There are songs for planting or harvesting crops. Songs are sung to the buffalo. When men cart heavy loads singing helps ease their burden. Fishermen sing as they row out to sea for the daily catch, they sing to the turtles and dolphins and to the nautilus shells before they take them to decorate their traditional houses. Songs are sung when grinding grain, the rhythmic accompaniment kept by the regular beat of the pounding poles or stones. Songs are sung to the trees before chopping them down to build houses.

Children sing songs in their games. One child leads, starting the melody and the other children join in singing the remainder of the song. There are songs for special ceremonies, such as during the building of the *uma lulik*, or for the hunting of the manta ray. Special songs are sung in the agricultural festivals. In the past, Timorese sang songs to welcome warriors home from battle.

Songs of death honour those who have died. The lyrics are topical, recounting stories about the deceased, and tell the history of that person's clan. The singing goes on day and night until the whole story is told. Precise detail is important, so that no harm will come to the deceased's spirit or to the remaining clan members. The singing also serves the purpose of guiding the spirit in its journey back to the "grandfather."[32] The grandfather referred to here is a generic term.

Song accompanies the *dahur*. The rhythm of the song provides a steady pulse for the dancers. The melodic material is usually diatonic (that is, using notes of a specific key, for example C major - C, D, E, F, G, A, B, C). Some melodies, however, are not diatonic, such as the *bidu tais mutin* from Suai which is accompanied by *raraun* and voice. In this *bidu* the vocalist sings a melody which may leap all over the place, have vibrato, ornamentation, slides and may even include yodelling and guttural sounds. In a typical *dahur* the melody is introduced by a caller (solo singer), either female or male. If male they might sing in a falsetto voice. The rest of the participants respond to the solo in chorus. It may be a male chorus followed by female chorus singing in a higher register, or a chorus sung by everyone. The chorus is often harmonised, in parallel 3rds, 4ths, 5ths or 6ths above the main melody, or sometimes singing in canon. Sometimes the melody is sung in unison with no harmonising.

NOTE The title of each song is followed by the original language of the lyrics. Only the melodic line of each song is notated in this book. The traditional songs selected are some of the lesser known ones and represent different aspects of traditional culture. These are in the language they were composed in, with translation provided in Tetun and English. The songs are on the CD. The songs are written in modern western musical notation and in the numerical system of notation familiar to many Timorese, which was introduced during the period of Indonesian occupation.

KNANANUK DANSA NIAN

Dahur Odi Makasae

Chorus	Chorus
ai nana lelele mata lo deu x 7	ele le le ele le laukai bala
solo	ele le o he le le le
o kulu mutu deda	hai-hai hai hala lai
deda kulu tula nawa wo	hai hala lai
	tutu ku ku oi...oi...oi

Dahur Odi mak knananuk ko'a hare. Tuir tradisaun, ema kanta nia bainhira hare prontu atu ko'a. 'Odi' signifika 'kulu' iha Makasae.

Dahur Odi is a harvest song. It is traditionally sung when the rice is ready to cut. *Odi* means breadfruit in Makasae.[33]

> EZEMPLU AUDIO husi Grupu Rebenta **CD TRACK/FAIXA 25**
> AUDIO EXAMPLE of *Dahur Odi* sung by Grupu Rebenta
> **CD TRACK 25**

O Mai Ita Tebe Tetun

O mai ita tebe
hele e le le le
hele hala ai o la le
maun alin sira o
mai ita tebe

Normalmente *tebedai* só dansa akompaña ho *baba dook* sira no *tala*. Iha mós knananuk iha *tebedai* ida ne'e.

Usually *tebedai* is only danced to the accompaniment of *baba dooks* and *tala*. However song as well as *baba dook* and *tala* accompany this *tebedai*.

> EZEMPLU AUDIO husi Grupu Rebenta **CD TRACK/FAIXA 32**
> AUDIO EXAMPLE of *O Mai ita Tebe* sung by Grupu Rebenta
> **CD TRACK 32**

DAHUR ODI

O MAI ITA TEBE

Ma i -ta te - be he - le e le le le he - le ha - la ai - o la

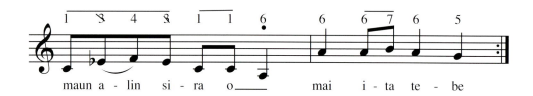

maun a - lin si - ra o____ mai i - ta te - be

TIKI O LÉ LÉ

Ti - ki o le - le ti-ki ka-ra bau o__ le - le ka-ra-ba-u la - ka o le - le la-ka te-u te-be o

le - le teu te-be teu Bau-kau o le - le Ba-u-ka-u we so-i ma-nu we soi o__ le - le

sa - e fa - su ba - e ba - e ma-nu ba - e bae o____ le

Tiki o lé lé Makasae

Tiki o lé lé
tiki karabau o lé lé
karabau laka o lé lé
laka teu tebe o lé lé
Baukau we soi
manu we soi o lé lé
sae fasu bae bae
manu bae bae o lé lé

Tiki o le le dansa ida hodi simu bainaka. Ida ne'e kanta bainhira halo uma-lulik, atu simu ema hotu ne'ebé mai selebrasaun.

Tiki o lé lé is a dance of welcome. It is sung when building the *uma lulik*, to welcome everyone to the celebration with singing and dancing.[34]

Boituka Makasae

Chorus
lo ele le oi ere lau   oli wai wai
buti tele gau   oli au oli were o
do loi la'a   ele bani o lo
ia.....ia.....   boy, boy olo
o...o...a....a....e.....e   boy o olo boy o

Boituka mak *tebedai* lulik ida ne'ebé mai husi foho Matebian ne'ebé kanta bainhira remata konstrusaun uma-lulik. Ema Makasae barak harii sira-nia uma-lulik iha foho Matebian.

Boituka iha fraze báziku rua, ne'ebé hatudu iha ezemplu muzikál. Soloista no koru troka malu no baibain koru repete sira-nia fraze. Soloista lidera knananuk ne'e no foti liafuan balu husi versu no halo modifíkasaun. Testu karik la tuir orden ne'ebé hakerek iha ne'e.

Boituka is a *lulik tebedai* from Mount Matebian which is sung when the *uma lulik* is finished. Many of the Makasae people build their *uma luliks* on Mount Matebian.[35]

Boituka has two basic phrases, as illustrated in the musical example. The soloist and chorus alternate and the chorus usually repeats their phrase. The soloist leads the song and takes some words from the verse given and varies it. The lyrics do not necessarily follow the order of the verse as written here.

BOITUKA

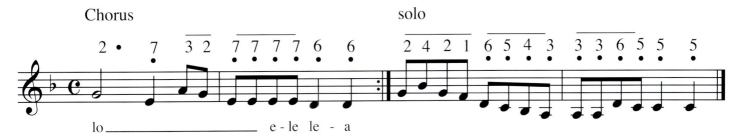

Semai Fataluku

Se... se... rolo mai a, se rolo roto, roto se rolo mai a...
Se... se... rolo mai a... no'o me mu'a tafa o se rolo mai a...

Se... se... rolo mai a... ca'u tote... mani tote halu na cote...
Se... sai se rolo ee... ca'u tote... mani tote... halu na cote...

Se... se... rolo mai a, se rolo roto, roto se rolo mai a...
Se... se... rolo mai a... no'o me mu'a tafa o se rolo mai a

Se... se... rolo mai a... ca'u me ulu cau o se rolo mai a...
Se... se... rolo mai a... ha'a kara mura nani o sai se rolo

Se... se... rolo mai a, se rolo roto, roto se rolo mai a...
Se... se... rolo mai a... no'o me mu'a tafa o se rolo mai a

Se sai se rolo ee... coro ho o at ia se rolo mai a
Se... se... rolo mai a... hoil ho furu ia se rolo mai a...
Se... se... rolo mai a, se rolo roto, roto se rolo mai a...
Se... se... rolo mai a... no'o me mu'a tafa o se rolo mai a...

Ne'e knananuk funu Fataluku nian ne'ebé tuan liu fali tempu kolonizasaun Portugál nian. Tribu sira ne'ebé viziñu dala ruma bá asalta knua seluk no na'ok riku soin no karau, bibi, fahi, ka manu sira. Nu'udar resposta ba ataka sira ne'e, funu na'in husi knua ne'e bá hadau fali sira-nia ema ida no lori fali mai. Iha ne'e inimigu nia kakorok sira taa no hasai ninia ulun. Depois sira tau ulun ne'e iha sírkulu nia klaran no sira dansa no kanta Semai.

This is a Fataluku war song from the time before Portuguese colonisation. Neighbouring tribes would sometimes raid each other's villages and steal riches such as livestock. In response to these attacks, warriors from the village invaded would go and take, as punishment, a member of the pillaging party and bring them back to their village. The offender's throat would be cut and the head removed. The men would then place the head on the ground, form a moving circle and sing this song, Semai.[36]

SEMAI

se ___ se ro - lo ___ mai - a se ro - lo ___ ro - to ro - to ___

se ro - lo ___ mai - a Se se ro - lo mai a ___

ca' ___ u ___ to - te ma - ni to - te ha - lu na ___ co - te se

sai se ro - lo ee ___ ca'u to - te ___ ma - ni to - te ha - lu na ___

co - te

Kelbeli Tokodede

Serimónia Kelbeli (ikan-pari)

o wailo
o wailo
o wailo
ae i la
wailo
o wailo

Dair knua ki'ik ida iha tasi ibun iha distritu Likisá. Ema Dair fiar katak sira iha relasaun espesiál ida ho tasi no rai. Tinan tinan, iha tempu ba sira atu kasa ikan-pari. Iha serimónia ida ba tempu ne'e. Serimónia ne'e tuan loos, no só sira mak halo, tuir lisan ne'ebé sira hatene husi bizavón sira. Kultura kelbeli ne'e mai husi avó ida naran Lekiseri.

Durante tempu kasa ikan-pari, mane ida ne'ebé bolu Ivu Lama mak bolu kelbeli. Kelbeli konsidera nu'udar buat lulik ida. Ró espesiál tolu mak bá kasa nia. Ró sira ne'e bolu Ese-Mau Mekei, Manu-Tasi Mekei, no Toda-Balu Mekei. Mane sira ne'ebé hean ró sira ne'e bolu Durumudi, Marineru, no Durawatu. Durawatu mós oho ikan-pari. Mane sira kanta knananuk Wailo bainhira sira kasa. To'o fali tasi ninin, sira oho ikan-pari iha fatuk espesiál ida nia leten. Fatuk ne'e bolu biti a'e, no ninia forma mak hanesan ho ikan-pari. Serimónia kontinua, no ema mama bua-malus, hemu, no han hahán kapás hodi selebra okaziaun ne'e.

Durante tempu Indonézia, ema barak iha Dair laran mak suporta Fretilin no Falintil sira. Ne'e mak Bapa sira estraga ró sira ne'ebé sira uza hodi kasa ikan-pari. Iha 2010, ho ajuda husi governu, povu Dair konsege halo tan ró espesiál ida, mak seremónia kasa ikan-pari komesa moris fali ona.

Tebe Makili Makili

Mane sira husi Makili (Ataúru) hananu knananuk importante ida ne'e bainhira sira halo ró tradisionál. Bainhira ema rona knananuk ne'e, sira hatene katak tempu to'o ona atu taa ai boot no dada mai husi foho.

Mane sira sa'e ba foho hodi taa ai ne'e no ko'a ninia forma. Tuir mai sira dada nia tun mai tasi, ba fatin ida naran *Tuli Peun*, mak sira remata knaar iha ne'ebá. Ai ne'ebé uza ne'e tipu ai-mean ida, naran lero.

Tebe Makili sei kanta to'o ohin loron. Bele mós kanta ba okaziaun seluk, maibé knananuk ne'e nia signifikadu klaru ona.

KELBELI

o __ wa-ilo __ o __ wa - ilo o __ wa-ilo ae i __ la __ wa - ilo o __ wa - ilo

TEBE MAKILI

Solo
u oi mose topokgahon
ta'a ngek mam-aun
oi mose topokgahon
ta'a ngek mam-aun u

Chorus
Kla'a hane Tuli Peun
kla'a aso peune
kla'a aso peune

Solo
Topo resa memouran
lero memouran
lero memouran

Chorus
ta'a kero meti noro
tahan meti noro
tahan meti noro

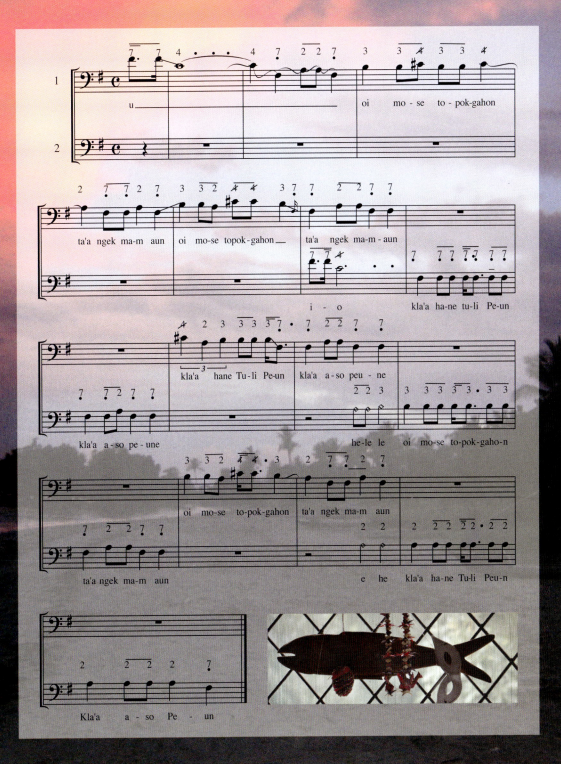

135

Kelbeli   Tokodede

The ceremony of *kelbeli* (manta ray)

o wailo
o wailo
o wailo
ae i la
wailo
o wailo

Dair is a small seaside village located in the Likisá district. The people of Dair believe they have a special connection to the sea and the land. At a certain time of the year they hunt the *kelbeli*. There is a specific ritualistic ceremony during which the *kelbeli* is caught and killed. This ceremony is an ancient tradition unique to the Dair, and passed onto the people by their ancestors. The *kelbeli* culture is believed to have come from the *avó* (grandparent) called *Lekiseri*.[37]

During the *kelbeli* hunting season, a man whose official title is *Ivu Lama* calls the *kelbeli*. *Kelbeli* is regarded as *lulik*. Three special boats are used for the hunt, called *Ɛse-Mau Mekei, Manu-Tasi Mekei* and *Toda-Balu Mekei*. The men who row the boats also have special titles, *Durumudi, Marinero* and *Durawatu*. *Durawatu* also kills the *kelbeli*. This song is sung by the men as they hunt the *kelbeli*. When the *kelbeli* is brought back to shore it is taken and killed on the special stone mat called *biti a'e*, which has a shape similar to the *kelbeli*. The ceremony continues, with much betel nut chewing and feasting.

During Indonesian times there were many people in Dair who supported the resistance, so in retribution the Indonesians destroyed the special boats used to hunt the *kelbeli*. In 2010 with the help of funding from the government, the people of Dair were able to build one of these special boats, enabling a rekindling of the ceremony associated with the hunting of the *kelbeli*.

AUDIO EXAMPLE of *Kelbeli* sung by men from Dair **CD TRACK 26**
AUDIO EXAMPLE of *Tebe Makili* sung by men of Makili **CD TRACK 36**

Tebe Makili Makili

Solo	Chorus	Solo	Chorus
u oi mose topokgahon	Kla'a hane Tuli Peun	Topo resa memouran	ta'a kero meti noro
ta'a ngek mam-aun	kla'a aso peune	lero memouran	tahan meti noro
oi mose topokgahon	kla'a aso peune	lero memouran	tahan meti noro
ta'a ngek mam-aun u			

Tebe Makili is a song of some importance, sung as part of the ritual involved in the making of the traditional fishing boats by the men of Makili. When people hear the song being sung, they know it is the signal that it is time to "*taa ai*" (cut the tree) and drag a boat from the mountains.[38]

The men go to the mountains to cut the wood and make the basic shape of the boat. Then they drag it to the sea, to the place known as *Tuli Peun* where they complete the making of the boat. The wood used is a red wood called *lero*, grown in the mountains.[39]

Tebe Makili is still sung today. It may be sung for other occasions, but essentially the song is associated with the making and dragging of the boat to the sea.

Inbeluk   Tetun Terik

ita soe lakon
ina ha'u we e hele o hele ha'u o (lao o)
e hele lao ha'u we e o le(le o lao o)

ita soe lakon
rai rai ina ina dulur e le (le)
taka ro... ho soe lakon kadeli
noho nain ne....... o.hele o hele la hau o

Ina wai-wain wain klakar
dulur e he (dulur) ina sa kola la'o hamutuk
wain o e hele o hele hau o
el le la'o o el le la

ina belu e le ha'u o ina mara sa kola
to'o we lae o ha'u we e ho e e
hele ho hele ha'u o hele la
ina mara sa kola o e la e

Inbeluk ne'e knananuk família ne'ebé kanta bainhira ema mate. Bainhira ema ida mate iha knua laran, knaar importante ne'ebé ema sei halo ba dahuluk mak fai batar no foos. Feto sira kanta knananuk ne'e bainhira fai batar no foos atu sente serbisu kmaan no halo sira sente kbi'it no ksolok. Komu knananuk ne'e iha relasaun ho membru família ne'ebé sira hadomi, kanta ne'e mai husi fuan duni. Knananuk ne'e mós kanta bainhira han nu'udar parte serimónia mate-nian. Kanta mós bainhira halo uma ka halo uma-lulik.

Inbeluk is a family song and sung as part of the celebrations for the dead. When someone dies in a village, one of the first tasks is to pound the corn and rice, which will be part of the feast for the ceremony. This song is sung as the women pound the grain to ease the monotony of the work and to make them strong and happy. As the song has its associations with the death of a loved one, the singing comes from the heart. This song is also sung at the beginning of the feasting as part of the funeral ceremony. It is also sung when the family is building their house or for the building of the uma lulik.

Lolan   Bunak

Lolan neé gole Maubesi
wa uen loren koen
Han loren koen
Lolan gol han lolen koen lolan gol

Lolan neé gole nona Atambua nona galzal ua
Han gazal lolan gole han gazal ua lolan gol

Lolan neé gole muk, mugi mau na gaba loi
Han gaba loil lolan gol han gaban loi lolan gol

Lolan mak knananuk Bunak ba hakoi mate-isin, husi Lolotoe. Só kanta durante tempu kakeker ka lutu nia laran no iha fatin balu de'it mak sei uza. Família no kolega sira husi Matebian mak kanta, konta hela moris Matebian nian no asegura nia katak 'sira sei hasoru malu filafali iha mundu seluk ne'ebá.'

Lolan is a Bunak funeral song from the Lolotoe district, sung only during the period of mourning and is only sung in a few places now. The mourners sing the song, which describes the life of the person who has just died, and assures them that they will meet again in the after life.

INBELUK

EZEMPLU AUDIO *Inbeluk* kanta husi feto sira husi Suai Loro
CD TRACK/FAIXA 35

AUDIO EXAMPLE *Inbeluk* sung by women from Suai Loro
CD TRACK 35

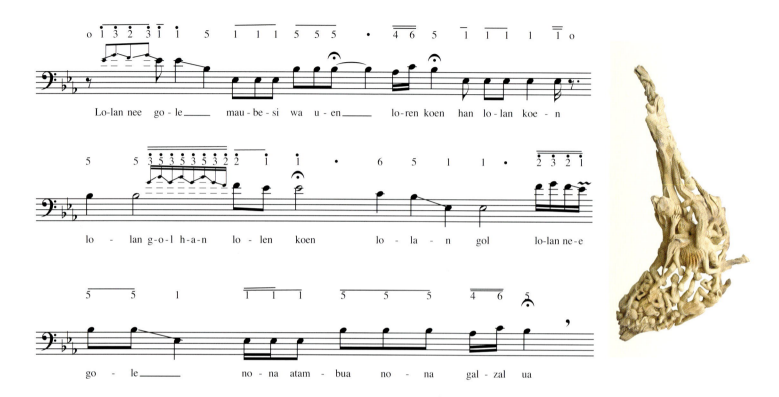

Lo-lan nee go-le____ mau-be-si wa u-en____ lo-ren koen han lo-lan koe-n

lo- lan g-o-l h-a-n lo-len koen lo- la-n gol lo-lan ne-e

go- le____ no-na atam-bua no- na gal-zal ua

Pankalalále Baikeno

Pankalalále mak knananuk ida ne'ebé kanta bainhira fai foos iha manko ai hodi prepara hahan iha mate uma. Ida ne'e halo antes hakoi mate-isin.

La iha diferensa boot entre koru no versu kompara ho knananuk seluk husi tipu bonet. Parese liafuan sira muda dala ba dala maski ema ne'ebé hanesan mak kanta.

EZEMPLU AUDIO husi Pasquela Eko no populasaun sira iha Kutet, Oekusi CD TRACK/FAIXA 33
AUDIO EXAMPLE *Pankalalále* CD TRACK 33

The *Pankalalále* is the chant sung when pounding rice in a wooden trough for the funeral banquet of the deceased. The pounding is done before the burial, when the deceased is still present.

The chorus and verse of the *Pankalalále* is not as distinguishable as in other *bonet* genre chants. It seems that the words vary from performance to performance even when sung by the same person. Pasquela Eko, who sings the *Pankalalále* on the CD recording, sings different words to those she sang for Richard Daschbach when he transcribed her singing. That version can be found in the chapter on Oekusi.

PANKALALÁLE

Pankalalále e-i
o le manu nani ko beti
o le manu nani ko beti
o..o..le..
o le o le kal koi
ai maun belu ba,
e maun sa la la, la la la la.

O Seiki nameu na man,
ai manu nako nai jan.
Pankalalále nao nako me.

Nao nako ia ma-o ma-e.
La le mulai hau bakan fi la le i.

Mnao kum bae, mfain kum bae,
sia la sia le lo hai on i.

Le bae toli kase,
le bau toli kaesle hais e nuen.
Hais e nuen ana lou.

Lou lou ak ko san.
Sala nunbai tunan
tun ana le mumnau nekma bae.

Lolu ak sala
ahoe,ho-e kita le kol, akbali bae.

Mnao kum bae, mfain kum bae,
sia la sia le lo hai on i.

Ai Lolole Fataluku

Ai lo lo le, sa lo lo le… kene-kene taya. Na'u kene taya…
Ai lo lo le, sa lo lo le… kene-kene taya. Na'u kene taya…

Moco pal upen l'e na'u kene taya, kene-kene taya. Na'u kene taya

Ai lo lo le, sa lo lo le   Na'u kene taya… kene-kene taya
Ai lo lo le, sa lo lo le. Na'u kene taya… kene-kene taya

Pala hai la'a apa tali molu, nala hai la'a ili tali molu
Pua raka petel oo na'u kene taya, lauluka petel oo, kene-kene taya
Ai lo lo le, sa lo lo le… kene-kene taya. Na'u kene taya…
Ai lo lo le, sa lo lo le… kene-kene taya. Na'u kene taya…

Pala hai la'a ira tali molu, nala hai la'a veru tali molu…
Moco pal upen ie naukene taya. Moco nalu palin ie kene-kene taya…
Omoke nu taya, na'u kene taya, kene-kene taya, tepere nu taya…

Ai Lolole mak knananuk fataluku nian ida ne'ebé uza hodi hatoba labarik ki'ik.

Ha'u halo o sente di'ak. Toba ona bá…
Amá no Apá matan dukur ona
Agora ó ho ha'u, ita maun alin
 Amá no Apá sei fila mai lailais.
Toba, toba nonok
Amá bá to'os atu foti ai-han ruma
Apá sa'e foho atu kuru bé
Nonok, toba ona bá…
Amá no Apá sei fila mai lailais, keta hanoin barak

EZEMPLU AUDIO *Ai Lolole* anta husi Osme Gonçalves
CD TRACK/FAIXA 23

Ai Lolole is a Fataluku lullaby.

I make you comfortable, please sleep
Mummy and Daddy need to sleep
Now you are with me, you and I are brothers.
Mummy and Daddy will be back soon,
sleep, sleep quietly.
Mummy is going to the garden to get some food for us,
Daddy is going to the mountain to get water for us,
please sleep, be quiet.
Mummy and Daddy will be back soon, don't worry.

AUDIO EXAMPLE *Ai Lolole* sung by Osme Gonçalves
CD TRACK 23

Lela Gie Gol Bunak

lai lai hali lai hali lai hali lai
sama nasik e ai asik e
o zemal da no ai hani hani zoin
nei gozol zoin gie aiba oma nii

tebe selele o hele la
o le lombete kasian bete lai

lai lai hali lai hali lai hali lai
sama nasik e ai asik e
birul nala talo ai neto hui
hui neto die reu aiba sae nii
tebe sele le o hele la
o le lombete kasian bete lai

Lela gie gol knananuk namora kona-ba feto raan sira husi Lela. Ida ne'e kanta iha Lolatoe, Lebos, no Gildapil iha distritu Bobonaru.

Lela Gie Gol is a courtship song about the girls from Lela, and is sung in the Bobonaru villages of Lolotoe, Lebos and Gildapil.

AI LOLOLE

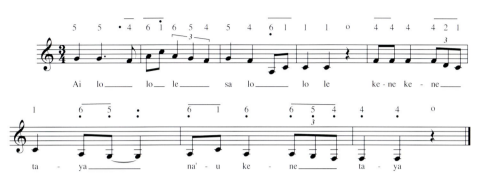

LELA GIE GOL

Vetere (muhal makua)
Ancient Fataluku

meci nal a kuru mucu nu'ute marite
a uru-uru a poko-poko

kinamoko usuroit emere nu ma'u
a tapa usuroi ina taka-taka

una-uname a, meci name a
una-uname a, meci name a

capaku sauke meci sauke a
capaku sauke meci sauke a

Ehe vetere dala mai o lele sekur
ehe Puiyoho'o ira mucu puiserar o

ira mucu asena vari fala asa sai o
vari fala-mire janetiti jani e na rei-rei

asino rei-rei asi e na tarei-rei
ira mucu asena vari fala asa sai o

vari fala mirejanetiti jani e na rei-rei
asino rei-rei asi e na tarei-rei

Muhal Makua (lovaia epul)

metxi: kaer nia hodi han

Vetere kanta molok atu bá kasa metxi, mak ular tasi tipu ida. Ida ne'e konta istória metxi nian. Dansa espesiál ida mós iha, ne'ebé akompaña knananuk ne'e. Mane ida husi knua ne'e la'o tama tasi atu hare'e metxi iha ka seidauk. Kuandu iha, nia bolu, "metxi hai mau" (metxi iha ne'e no sei mai tan) mak ema hotu halai bá kaer sira. Atu bolu metxi, povu sira dehan "uh metxi o!" Versaun iha CD laran modernu, maibé uluk nia hanesan sani duké knananuk.

Vetere is sung before hunting *metxi* (sea worm). It tells the story of the *metxi*. There is also a special dance that goes with this song. One man in the village wades out in the sea to see if there are *metxi*. If there are, he calls out to everyone else "*metxi hai mau*" (*metxi* are here and coming) then everyone goes out to catch them. To call the *metxi* the people say "*uh metxi o!*" [40] The arrangement on the CD has been modernised from the original, which is more chanted than sung.

Txai Telu Fataluku

Txai Telu, Telu Nami Namirara eh
Txai Telu, Telu Nami Pal afur eh. x 2

Lutur a tu mu'a ta'a-ta'ane ra
Rah itu Kotxo kuruk a'ape a ta ta'a.

Txiri ho e Txalu a tu i atxu txuale ra.
Txiri ho e Txalu a tui mini txuale ra.

Lutur a tu mu'a ta'a-ta'ane ra
Rah itu Kotxo kuruk a'ape a ta ta'a.

Nere natxin hai pali Txai Telu eh
Nere txoton hai pali pal afur eh

En i it e upen i ho molun txipi-txipi i ra
En i it e upen i ho e molun utxu-patxu i ra

TXAI TELU

Txai Telu knananuk 'tanis' nian. Nia kona-ba mane ida naran Txai Telu ne'ebé sai husi ninia knua atu bá funu. Txai Telu nunka fila, entaun ninia alin feto bá fatin barak hodi buka nia, bolu hela ninia naran. Nia kanta knananuk ida ne'e durante nia buka ninia maun.

Txai Telu is a 'crying song'. It is about a man called Txai Telu who left his village to go off to war. Txai Telu never returned so his little sister went from place to place looking for him and calling his name. She sang this song while looking for her elder brother.[41]

AUDIO EZEMPLU *Vetere* kanta husi Etson Caminha, Adilson Arintis da Costa Caminha, Ananias Carlos no Alfeo Sanches Pereira CD FAIXA/TRACK 40

EZEMPLU AUDIO *Txai Telu* kanta husi Luciano Gonçalves CD TRACK/FAIXA 39 AUDIO EXAMPLE of *Txai Telu,* sung by Luciano Gonçalves CD TRACK 39

Tupukur ulute Ancient Fataluku

Tupukur ulute
rulu ina maite
ina mata pua tei
pua-saka ta'te
kei-keililino lele valu-valuno
lele nita pokite, poki nita kaite

Ce oioile Cama oioile
Ce ciri ko'ko, Cama ciri ko'ko
Kaile, kakile, kesume, em ura

Cura valikasa sei-seile
Napu valikasa sei-seile
Cura o e vali tene tote
Napu o e vali tene tote
Kaile, kakile, kesume, em ura

Cele cuku, cele cuku, leu ta'tate
Leu ta'tate, poko ta'tate
Kaile, kakile, kesume, em ura

Tupukur ulute nia signifikadu loos lakon ona, maski labarik sira iha Lautein sei kanta ezatamente hanesan ne'e dezde uluk kedas. Liafuan sira ne'e Fataluku antigu ne'ebé ema la kolia ona. Labarik sira tuur iha sírkulu no halimar jogus ho sira-nia liman fuan hodi marka ritmu bainhira kanta knananuk ida ne'e. Depois sira buti tilun, no kaer malu iha tilun, bainhira muda uitaon no kontinua kanta.

Tuir istória ida, kakuuk ida subar an iha fatin nakukun ne'ebé mós diabu uza hodi subar. Labarik sira ta'uk ho kakuuk ne'e, entaun sira kaer sira-nia tilun no kanta atu lalika ta'uk demais. Orijinalmente Tupukur Ulute loloos sani, la'os knananuk, no sei hatudu hanesan ne'e iha distritu Lautein. Iha CD nia laran, ita rona sani hafoin versaun knananuk hahú, ne'ebé múziku balu husi Lospalos mak inventa.

The meaning of the *Tupukur ulute* has been lost, even though the people of Lautein have sung it verbatim from childhood since ancient times. The language of the song is an ancient form of Fataluku, which people in Lautein today do not speak. When children sing this song, they sit in a circle and do finger games in time to the beat as they sing. Later they tweak their ears and hold one another's ears, as they move and sing the rest of the song.

One story goes that the owl hides in a dark place where the devil is thought to be hiding too. The children are afraid of the owl and they hold their ears and fingers and sing so they won't be afraid.[42] Originally *Tupukur ulute* was more a chant than a song, and is still performed as such in Lautein district. The track on the CD begins with the chant and then the sung version, which some musicians from Lospalos have created.

Lifau Baikeno

Lifau Lifau o Lifau	Lifau Lifau o Lifau
Ambeno in hun	Ambeno in hun
Lifau Lifau o Lifau	Lifau Lifau o Lifau
alako alako Lifau	alako alako Lifau
Laes un unu napun nanko	Masi onle i ho kamumas
Laes amunit ambet nanko	ala ho kanam esambolpan
masi onle nan Ambeno	masi onle nan Ambeno
ala he ta uiski tala neno i	fe nahinkit tala neno i
alako alako alako Lifau	alako alako alako lifau
Masi onle i ho kamumas	Lifau Lifau o Lifau
ala ho kanam esambolpan	Ambeno in hun
	Lifau Lifau o Lifau
fe nahinkit tala neno i	alako alako Lifau
alako alako alako Lifau	alako alako Lifau

AUDIO EZEMPLU/AUDIO EXAMPLE *Tupukur ulute* sani husi/chant by Etelevina Dos Santos kanta husi/sung by Etson Caminha, Adilson Arintis da Costa Caminha, Ananias Carlos, Alfeo Sanches Pereira CD TRACK/FAIXA 38

TUPUKUR ULUTE

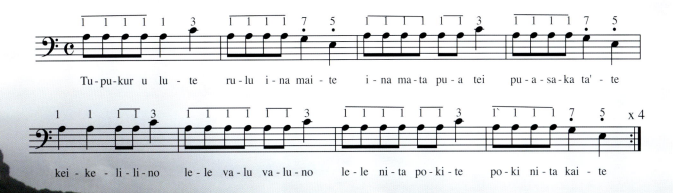

LIFAU

Lifau mak fatin ne'ebé Portugés sira monu ain ba dahuluk iha nusa Timor iha sékulu 16. Tuir istória, naran Lifau signifika 'liat namfau ntolan nbin' ka 'kolega barak hasoru malu iha ne'e.' Knananuk ne'e kona-ba Lifau, sentru Ambenu nian, ne'ebé koñesidu no respeitadu to'o agora. "Lifau, o di'ak liu!"

Lifau is the place where the Portuguese first set foot on Timor at the beginning of the sixteenth century. Hearsay is, that the word *Lifau* came from a collation of the words *Liat namfau ntolan nbin!* (many friends met there). The song tells how *Lifau*, Ambenu's centre, is famous and still well known and admired to the present day. "How good you are, *Lifau!*" [43]

AUDIO EZEMPLU *Lifau* kanta husi estudante sira husi Eskola Secondaria Oekusi CD TRACK/FAIXA 28
AUDIO EXAMPLE of *Lifau* sung by Students of Eskola Secondaria Oekusi CD TRACK 28

KNANANUK HO LAKADOU

Lila ho le Mambae

Lila ho le lila ho lei
Lila ho loi batu lila ho loi laran x 2

Lila ho le hele lila ho lei
Lila ho loi batu lila ho loi laran x 2

Lila ho le hele lila ho lei
se temi temi to'o tan ona

Lila ho le hele lila ho lei
Si goi tali tan to tan ona

Lila ho le lila ho lei
Lila ho loi batu lila ho loi laran x 2

Lila ho le hele lila ho lei
Lila ho loi batu lila ho loi laran x 2

Knananuk Mambae ida ne'e kanta ho *lakadou*, tuir tradisaun.

AUDIO EZEMPLU *Lila ho le* labarik sira husi grupu
Holarua CD TRACK/FAIXA 29

This Mambae song is traditionally sung with the *lakadou* played
as an accompaniment.

AUDIO EXAMPLE *Lila ho le*, sung by children from
Grupu Holarua CD TRACK 29

LILA HO LE

O Maria Mambae/Tetun

Maria ho ninia laen iha to'os ne'ebé dook liu. Loroloron, sira bá haree to'os ne'e. Maria kanta knananuk ida ne'e bainhira ninia laen bá defende to'os ne'e husi lekirauk sira ne'ebé atu estraga sira- nia to'os.

NOTA Iha Same, ema sei ta'uk uitoan ho lekriauk sira. Iha istória ida dehan katak iha labarik mane ida ne'ebé fila an ba lekirauk. Loron ida, ninia amá tau matan ba sira-nia to'os maibé nia matan dukur tiha. Durante momentu ne'e nia iha relasaun ruma ho lekirauk no nia isin rua! Depois, nia hahoris lekirauk nia oan mane. Ema ne'ebá sempre hetan problema ho labarik ne'e tamba nia nakar teen.

Ema balu fiar katak istória ne'e loos duni no labarik mane-lekirauk ne'e sei moris hela, maibé balu hanoin katak ne'e ai-knanoik de'it.

Maria and her husband have a field far, far away. Everyday, they go and look after their field. Maria sang this song when her husband went to guard the farm to stop the monkeys destroying their field.

NOTE In Same the monkey is regarded with suspicion. The story goes that there was a boy who became a monkey. One day his mother was looking after the farm and she fell asleep. While she was asleep she had a relationship with a monkey and had a monkey's baby boy. The people in this area always struggled with this boy because he caused trouble.

Some people believe this story to be true and that this monkey boy is alive, others consider it to be a fairy tale.

Chorus
Kru batar hin kai buti
Maria bali leura
Maria lain tara hauta maria o lele x 2

o helele ----- oh helela

Verse 1
konlisensa nai ulun ami tebe lai
ami tebe ho hananu solok imi laran

Chorus

Verse 2
Ami tuur rai Timor tetuk be tetuk
hakruk manu Timor manu be malae

Chorus

Verse 3
rai oan namkari lemo to'o rai hotu
temi kona hali hun
fila bá o nia fatin
brrrrrrrrrrrr

Chorus

Verse 4
Halibur hamutuk ita ida de'it
kaer liman ba malu foti ita rai

Chorus

OH MARIA

kru ba-tar hin kai bu-ti Ma-ri-a ba-li le-u-ra___ Ma-ri-a la-in ta-ra hau-ta Ma-ri-a o le-le

o he-le le oh he-le la Kon-li-sen-sa nai u-lun a-mi te-be la-i a-mi te-be ho ha-nan-u

so-lok i - mi la - ran

GLOSÁRIU

ailoos
Ai-pedasuk rua ne'ebé hatuur iha kelen leten. Tokadór tuur no baku ai-pedasuk sira ne'e ho ai-tanutuk rua. Toka hamutuk ho dansa bidu *ailoos*, distritu Kovalima nian.

au
Au loos, silindru ida. Huu mak halo lian.

aul noni
Baikeno
Kohe ne'ebé hale'u ho sinu ki'ik sira ka osan-besi, uza iha bsoot iha Oekusi. Ninia lian kontribui ba ritmu.

baba
Termu jerál ba *tambór*.

baba dook
Tambór ki'ik ne'ebé ita tara ka habit iha ita-nia kabaas okos. Uza hodi akompaña dansa, porezemplu *tebedai*.

baba dook ki'ik
Hanesan *baba dook* maibé ninia tamañu ki'ik liután.

babuk
Kelu ain ne'ebé nakdoko bá-mai no halo husi au. Uza iha *bidu ailoos*.

baikeno
Lian ne'ebé uza iha Oekusi.

bano
Baikeno
Kelu ain halo husi birak ne'ebé kesi ho tali mahar no uza au hodi liga birak sira ne'e. Nia naruk besik metru ida no nia todan liu kilograma ida. Mai husi Oekusi.

bidu
Dansa tuir liña, baibain akompaña ho instrumentu.

bidu tais mutin
Dansa tuir liña, akompaña ho *raraun*. Ema sira ne'ebé dansa kaer salenda mutin iha sira-nia oin bainhira sira dansa.

bijol meto
Baikeno
Instrumentu ida ne'ebé ema halo rasik. Ne'e viola ki'ik ho tali haat dala barak ita bele hetan iha Oekusi no dala ruma mós ita bele hetan iha Ataúru.

bobakasa
Makasae
Tambór ulun rua.

bobakasa girte
Makasae
Ai-tanutuk ne'ebé uza hodi baku bobakasa.

bonet
Baikeno
Dansa tradisionál husi Oekusi ne'ebé akompaña ho múzika.

bsoot
Forma dansa livre husi Oekusi. Ema ne'ebé dansa tara *bano* Baikeno (Kelu ain halo husi birak) iha sira-nia ain-fukun. Sira halo sira-nia ritmu rasik hodi hamaluk *ke'e* no *sene*. Ne'e akompaña mós ho dansa.

cavaquinho
Portugés
Viola ho tali haat ne'ebé mai husi Portugál.

choro
Portugés
Tuir tradisaun ema bolu chorinho ka "tanis ki'ik" ou "halerik ki'ik." Instrumentu populár ne'e mai husi Brazil. Inventa iha Rio de Janeiru iha sékulu 19.

dadili
Makasae
Tala iha lian Makasae.

dahur
Dansa tradisionál Timor nian ho forma kabuar. Dansarinu sira kaer liman hamutuk, kanta, no tebe sira-nia ain bainhira sira dansa.

feku
Baikeno
Flauta ki'ik husi ai ne'ebé hetan iha foho iha rejiaun Timor-Osidentál.

inuh leko
Baikeno
Morteen (haree ninia esplikasaun iha morteen).

kaebauk
Enfeite ne'ebé tau iha ita-nia reen-toos ne'ebé halo husi osan-mutin, uza ho roupa tradisionál.

kafu'i
Flauta ne'ebé halo husi au ka ai, ninia boot iha variasaun husi sentímetru balu to'o metru 1.

kafu'i boot
Flauta au baixu, ninia medida kuaze sentímetru 80.

kafu'i ki'ik
Kafu'i lian aas, halo husi au, ninia naruk maizumenus sentímetru 65

kakalo
Fataluku
Tambór sakat ne'ebé halo husi au. Mai husi Lautein.

kakal'uta
Fataluku
Instrumentu ida ne'ebé halo husi ai-lolon ho forma hanesan silindru. Ninia son no ritmu atu hanesan ho marimba.

kakeit
Instrumentu ibun, dala ruma ema bolu jaw harp ka mouth harp iha lian inglés.

kantiga
Kanta ho melodia ne'ebé hanesan, hahú husi parte ne'ebé diferente atu nune'e bele hasara tuir no kontinua nafatin.

karau dikur
Halo husi karau nia dikur, ema uza ba okaziaun tradisionál.

kbola
Baikeno
Tala ne'ebé uza hodi marka tempu (atu lailais ka neineik) ne'ebé uza iha *tala* lubun iha Oekusi.

ke'e
Baikeno
Tambór ain haat ne'ebé mai husi Oekusi.

knobe
Baikeno
Instrumentu ibun. Iha lian Tetun bolu *kakeit*.

koke Fataluku	Instrumentu ibun ne'ebé uza iis, ne'ebé bobar husi au nia tahan, ho forma hanesan kone-sorvete.
kokotere	Instrumentu ida ho forma hanesan trombeta. Halo husi au no tali tahan. Ninia medida kuaze metru ida ho balu.
lakadou	Tubu ida ne'ebé halo husi au ho tali ne'ebé mós halo husi au.
leku sene Baikeno	Leku nia arti mak nia (feto) halimar. *Sene* nia arti mak *tala*. Nia mai husi Oekusi.
lelan Baikeno	Versaun husi *bsoot*, dansa ne'e aprezenta husi feto sira.
Lia Na'in	Ema respeitadu, normalmente mane ida ne'ebé tuan, ne'ebé kaer lisan, lidera serimónia sira, no ema hotu konsidera nia nu'udar autoridade kona-ba kultura no tradisaun.
likurai	Forma husi *tebedai*. Mai husi Kovalima. Liku nia arti mak doko parte leten husi ita-nia isin.
lulik	Sagradu, bei'ala sira-nia espíritu.
Makadade	Foho ne'ebé aas liu iha Ataúru.
Makasae	Lian ne'ebé uza iha distritu Baukau.
Makili	Lian ne'ebé uza iha Ataúru.
marimba Kimbundu, Dalen Bantu husi Afrika	*Xilofone* ne'ebé nia hun mai husi rai Áfrika (Dalen Bantu husi Afrika).
mortar Inglés	Iha lian Tetun bolu *lesun*. Uza hodi fai batar.
morteen	Morteen kór saburaka, hanesan kolár musamusan barak. Konsidera hanesan fatuk ne'ebé folin boot. Uza iha serimónia kazamentu. Ema fiar katak musamusan sira ne'e mai husi Índia no halo husi frasku ne'ebé ema halo nabeen.
Muitkase Baikeno	Futu-kabun mutin ne'ebé mai husi Oekusi. Mane sira uza futu-kabun ne'e hanesan parte husi roupa tradisionál.
noni bena Baikeno	Pedasuk osan-besi husi osan-mutin boot, belar no kabuar. Uza hanesan parte husi roupa tradisionál iha Oekusi.
noni funan Baikeno	Osan mutin ne'ebé forma hanesan fulan. Halo husi osan-besi husi osan-mutin no uza hanesan parte roupa tradisionál husi Oekusi.
niti noni Baikeno	Kelu osan mutin, halo husi osan-besi husi osan-mutin no uza hanesan parte husi roupa tradisionál Oekusi nian.
oilu Baikeno	Hena ne'ebé ema kesi iha ulun hanesan parte roupa tradisionál iha Oekusi.
pai koe-koe Fataluku	Instrumentu anin ne'ebé halo husi au nia tahan ne'ebé ema bobar no forma hanesan kone-sorvete. Ninia tamañu nato'on de'it. Nia objetivu prinsipál mak hodi duni fahi sira ne'ebé sei estraga no han ai-horis sira. Pai nia arti mak fahi, no koe-koe iha Fataluku signifika *lian ne'ebé fahi halo.*
paos ab noni Baikeno	Futu-kabun husi osan mutin halo husi noni bena, pedasuk boot no belar kabuar ne'ebé halo husi osan-besi husi osan-mutin. Uza hanesan parte roupa tradisionál Oekusi nian.
pestle Inglés	Instrumentu todan ho tutun kabuar. Ema uza hodi harahun ka fai batar. Iha Tetun bolu 'alu.' Alu nia funsaun seluk mak akompaña múzika hanesan ritmu ida.
rabeka mós violinu	Instrumentu múzika ho tali haat ne'ebé ema kaer iha timir ka hasahún okos hodi toka ho arku.
rai rai Waima	Instrumentu ibun, iha Inglés jaw harp ka mouth harp. Iha lian Tetun bolu *kakeit*.
rama	Instrumentu ibun ne'ebé halo husi rama-inan. Bele hetan iha Ataúru. Iha lian Inglés bolu Mouth Bow.
raraun Tetun Terik	*Gitarra* ki'ik ne'ebé uza tali 4. Hetan iha Kovalima no parte balu iha Timor-Osidentál. Iha lian Tetun bolu *viola*. Iha Timor- Osidentál bolu *bijola*.
sabalu noni Baikeno	Roupa tradisionál husi Oekusi. Hanesan kazaku ka kamiza ne'ebé liman laek no hale'u ho osan-besi barak. Ema hatais *sabalu noni* bainhira dansa bsoot. Sira halo lian ki'ik.
samba Portugés	Dansa Brazileiru nian.
sasando Rote dialect	Instrumentu múzika ne'ebé halo husi kaixa ai-kabelak ho tali barak. *Sasando* mai husi província Nusa Tenggara Timur, Indonézia.
sene Baikeno	*tala*
snarko Mambae	Instrumentu ibun ka mouth harp. Ema bolu *kakeit* iha lian Tetun.

soeb noni
Baikeno

Osan mutin ne'ebé sai hanesan parte roupa tradisionál husi Oekusi. Iha Tetun bolu kaebauk.

suni
Baikeno

Surik iha lian Baikeno.

tala

Instrumentu muzikál ida ne'ebé halo husi birak. Iha lian Inglés bolu gong. Ema uza iha *tebedai* hodi hamaluk *baba dook*. Normalmente *tala* nia parte klaran hasa'e aas uitoan no ninia ninin sira bele naruk ka kle'an.

tais

Hena mafutar ne'ebé halo parte ba kultura Timor nian.

tara bandu

Tara nia arti mak kesi ka tara sasán. Bandu nia arti mak buat ida ne'ebé uza atu identifika ema ka fatin ou fatin ne'e bandu. Nune'e tara bandu hanesan serimónia públika ida ne'ebé eziste hodi bandu populasaun atu labele estraga ema nia to'os ka taa ai arbiru. Bainhira ema ida la tuir desizaun ne'ebé foti tiha ona, nia sei hetan malisan.

tebedai
Baikeno

Dansa liña tradisionál ne'e akompaña husi *baba dook* no *tala*.

tefnai
Baikeno

Naran husi *tala* ida hanesan parte husi *tala* lubun iha dansa Oekusi nian.

tihak
Makili

Tambór boot. Bainhira ita uza instrumentu ne'e, ita hatoba ninia sorin ida iha ita-nia kelen leten.

toluk
Baikeno

Naran husi tala ida hanesan parte husi *tala* lubun ne'ebé ema uza iha Oekusi hodi akompaña dansa sira.

tohin

Tambór ho ulun ida, ho forma silindru boot. Normalmente nia hamriik iha rai.

ukulele
Hawaii

Instrumentu ki'ik ho tali lima. Ninia forma orijinál mai husi Portugál.

uma lulik

Uma ne'ebé ema uza hodi rai sasán lulik no fatin atu hamulak ba Matebian no bei'ala sira.

xilofone
Grésia

Instrumentu muzikál hanesan pianu ho tekla barak halo husi ai ne'ebé tokadór tuku ho ai-tanutuk rua.

zither
husi parte
Europa Leste

Instrumentu múzika ne'ebé halo husi kaixa ai-kabelak ho tali barak. Bele toka ho liman no mós bele uza objetu seluk, porezemplu ai-mihis ki'ik ka plástiku mihis ne'ebé bolu plektru ka *pick* iha lian Inglés.

GLOSSARY

ailoos

A percussive musical instrument: leg xylophone. Each player has two wooden keys laid across their legs which they strike with beaters. They accompany the dance *bidu ailoos*, a dance from Kovalima District.

aul noni
Baikeno

Bag with bells or coins attached, worn by dancers of the *bsoot* in Oekusi. The jingle of the coins contributes to the percussive rhythms.

au

Cylindrical bamboo wind instrument.

baba

Generic term for drum.

baba dook

Small drum held under the arm. It accompanies dances such as the *tebedai*.

baba dook ki'ik

Small *baba dook*.

tihak
Makili

Large drum laid sideways across the lap to play.

babuk

Bamboo ankle bells.

baku maka'as

To play strongly.

Baikeno

A language spoken in Oekusi.

bano

Brass ankle bells from Oekusi, looped together with thick rope and bamboo connectors, about a metre in length and several kilos in weight.

bidu

Line dance, usually accompanied by instruments.

bidu tais mutin

Line dance, accompanied by the *raraun*. The dancers hold a white woven cloth (*tais*) in front of them as they dance.

bijol meto
Baikeno

Home made ukelele, a small four stringed guitar, found predominantly in Oekusi and occasionally in Ataúro.

bobakasa
Makasae

Double-headed drum.

bobakasa girte
Makasae

Drum sticks for playing the *bobakasa*.

bonet
Baikeno

Traditional circle dance from Oekusi accompanied by song.

bsoot
Baikeno

Traditional dance from Oekusi accompanied by instruments.

cavaquinho
Portuguese

Four-stringed Portuguese guitar.

choro Portuguese	*Choro*, traditionally called *chorinho*, 'little cry' or 'little lament', is a Brazilian instrumental popular music style, with origins in nineteenth century Rio de Janeiro.
Canon	The same melody which is begun in different parts successively, so that the imitations overlap.
dadili Makasae	Gong.
dahur	Traditional Timorese circle dance. Dancers hold hands or place their arms around each other and sing and stamp their feet as they dance.
feku Baikeno	Small wooden flute-like instrument found in the mountain regions of West Timor.
kafu'i	Flute made of bamboo or wood, varying in size from a few centimetres to a meter.
kafu'i boot	Bass bamboo flute, about 80 cm in length.
kafu'i ki'ik	Alto *kafu'i*, made of bamboo, about 65 cm in length.
inuh leko Baikeno	*Morteen* beads (see description under *morteen*).
kaebauk	Silver headdress worn with traditional dress.
kakalo Fataluku	Bamboo slit drum from Lautein District.
kakal'uta Fataluku	Percussion instrument made of pair of pitched cylindrical tubes, similar in sound and rhythm to the marimba.
kakeit	Mouth instrument, otherwise known as a jaw harp or mouth harp.
karau dikur	Buffalo horn, blown on ceremonial occasions.
kbola Baikeno	The name of the timekeeper gongs played in the gong ensemble to accompany the dances of Oekusi.
ke'e Baikeno	Four-legged standing drum from Oekusi.
knobe Baikeno	Mouth instrument, a jaw harp or mouth harp. It is called *kakeit* in Tetun.
knua	Small village.
koke Fataluku	Small wind instrument made from tightly wound bamboo leaves, shaped into a cone.

kokotere	Trumpet-like instrument made of bamboo and palm leaf, about 1.5 m long.
lakadou	Tubed bamboo zither.
leku sene Baikeno	*Leku* means she plays. *Sene* means gongs and are played in Oekusi
lelan Baikeno	Version of the *bsoot* danced by women.
Lia Na'in	The keeper of the word, or custodian of the culture.
likurai	Form of the *tebedai*, danced in Kovalima and accompanied by instruments. *Liku* means to shake the upper body.
Liurai	King, chief or noble.
lulik	Sacred, holy, taboo, or having a supernatural quality. Spirit from ancestral roots.
Makadade	The highest mountain on the island of Ataúru.
Makasae	Language spoken in Baukau district.
Makili	Language spoken on Ataúru.
marimba Kimbundu - a Bantu Language	Deep-toned xylophone of African origin.
mortar	Hollowed-out receptacle made of wood that is used to crush grain.
morteen	Orange beaded necklace regarded as precious, is given as an exchange gift in weddings. The beads are thought to have come from India and are made from molten glass. The strand is divided by two Venetian glass beads and a metal bauble, representing unification of the male and female through marriage.
Muitkase Baikeno	White belt, worn by men as part of traditional dress in Oekusi.
noni bena Baikeno	Big flat round piece of silver made up of silver coins, worn as part of traditional dress in Oekusi.
noni funan Baikeno	A silver moon, made up of silver coins and worn as part of the traditional dress of Oekusi.
niti noni Baikeno	Silver bracelet, made of silver coins and worn as part of traditional dress in Oekusi.

oilu Baikeno	Cloth headdress worn as part of traditional dress in Oekusi.
pai koe-koe Fataluku	Medium-sized wind instrument made of tightly wound bamboo leaves shaped into a cone. Its main purpose was to scare the pigs from eating the crops. *Pai* means pig, and *koe-koe* is the sound the pig makes expressed in Fataluku.
paos ab noni Baikeno	Silver belt made up of *noni bena*, the big flat and round pieces of silver. Worn in traditional dress in Oekusi.
pestle	Heavy tool with a rounded end used for crushing, pounding and grinding grain. Doubles as rhythm accompaniment to singing.
rabeka mós violinu	Violin.
rai rai Waima	Mouth instrument, a jaw harp or mouth harp. It is called *kakeit* in Tetun.
rama	Musical mouth bow, found on the island of Ataúru.
raraun Tetun Terik	Homemade four-stringed guitar, found in Kovalima and West Timor. It is known in Tetun as *biola*. In West Timor it is called *bijola*.
sabalu noni Baikeno	Traditional dress from Oekusi: vest with coins all over it, worn when dancing the *bsoot*. They provide a jangling sound.
samba Portuguese	Brazilian dance, in 2/4 time.
sasando Rote dialect	Tubed zither from the Nusa Tenggara Timur province of Indonesia.
sene Baikeno	Gong.
snarko Mambae	Mouth instrument, a jaw harp or mouth harp. It is called *kakeit* in Tetun.
soeb noni Baikeno	Silver crown, part of the traditional dress in Oekusi.
suni Baikeno	Sword.
tala	Gong in the Tetun language. Gongs in East Timor are mostly bossed, meaning that the centre of the gong is raised, while the rim can be shallow or deep.
tais	Traditional Timorese weaving.

tara bandu	*Tara* : Means the rock, or to hang things. *Bandu* : Something that identifies the place and people, a forbidden place. Thus to hang up items via a public ceremony to show that it is for now forbidden to chop trees or harvest a crop in that area; those who break the prohibition come under a curse.
tebedai Baikeno	Traditional line dance accompanied by drums and gongs. Sometimes elaborately choreographed.
tefnai Baikeno	The name of one of the pair of gongs played as part of the gong ensemble in Oekusi to accompany dances.
tihak Makili	Large drum laid sideways across the lap to play.
toluk Baikeno	The name of the single gong played as part of the gong ensemble in Oekusi to accompany dances.
tohin	Large, cylindrical, single-headed drum that mostly sits on the ground.
ukulele Hawaii	From Hawaii, small five-stringed instrument with origins in Portugal.
uma lulik	Traditional sacred house.
Xefe Suku	The village leader. Elected by the people of the village as the person responsible to the District Administrator.
xylophone Greek	Musical instrument consisting of tuned wooden bars on a frame played with mallets.
zither Folk - Eastern European	Musical instrument consisting of a flat wooden sound box with numerous strings stretched across it, played with fingers or a plectrum.

NOTES

1 Forbes, H.O. 1885, *A Naturalist's Wanderings in the Eastern Archipelago: A narrative of Travel and Exploration from 1878 to 1883*, Samson Low, Marston, Searle, & Rivington, London, p.424.

2 King, M. 1963, *Eden To Paradise*, Hodder and Stoughton, London, p.140.

3 Byrne, L. 1998, *Tata-hateke ba dok: Grandfather Looking For The Future*, CD, Tradisom records/Ministerio de Culturo, Portugal, p.86.

4 Kartomi, M. 2000, *Music of Timor, CD, Celestial Harmonies*, Tucson, p.23.

5 Hastanto, S. 2007, *Asia-Pacific Database on Intangible Cultural Heritage:Performing Arts:Sasando*, viewed 21 April, 2011, <http://www.accu.or.jp/ich/en/arts/A_IDN9.html>

6 Gomes, E.L. 2009, *Timor Leste Heartland: The Journey, Revolutionary Poems (16 pieces)*, Melbourne, viewed 20 March, 2011, <http://timorlesteheartland.com/Poems.html>

7 King, M. 1963, *Eden to Paradise*, Hodder and Stoughton, London, p.130.

8 The influence of the Portuguese is perhaps evident in the resemblance between the raraun and the cavaquinho, a four-stringed Portuguese guitar, used in choro and samba music.

9 Daschbach, R. Personal communication, 20 February, 2012.

10 Daschbach, R. Personal communication, 20 February, 2012.

11 Daschbach, R. Personal communication, 20 February, 2012.

12 Daschbach, R. Personal communication, 20 February, 2012.

13 Daschbach, R. Personal communication, 20 February, 2012.

14 Daschbach, R. Personal communication, 20 February, 2012.

15 Daschbach, R. Personal communication, 20 February, 2012.

16 The betel-nut consists of the manus leaves or catkins, which grow on vines; and the puah nut which grows at the top of a long slender palm-like tree. The nuts grow in bunches, called ki'i. When the nuts are still very tender and unripe, they are called puah klus.

17 Trindade, J. 2011, 'Lulik: The Core of Timorese Values,' paper presented at: Communicating New Research on Timor-Leste, third Timor-Leste Study Association Conference, Dili, East Timor, 30th June-1st July.

18 Traube, E. 1986, *Cosmology and Social Life: Ritual Exchange among the Mambai of East Timor,* University of Chicago Press, Chicago. p.11.

19 King, M. 1963, *Eden to Paradise*, Hodder and Stoughton, London, p.134.

20 Byrne, L. 1998, 'Aman Ba Oan: getting inside the belly of the crocodile', BArts [Hons] Thesis, Deakin University, Melbourne, p. 7.

21 Sarmento, E. Information on Mythology, instruments, Personal communication, 5 July, 2010.

22 Traube, E. 1986, *Cosmology and Social Life: Ritual Exchange among the Mambai of East Timor*, University of Chicago Press, Chicago. p.159.

23 Sarmento, E. Information on Mythology, instruments, Personal communication, 5 July, 2010.

24 Pereira, M. Tohin, information, Personal communication, 16 April, 2004.

25 Pereira, J. Titir, Popokasa, Personal communication, 15 November, 2011.

26 King, M. 1963, *Eden to Paradise*, Hodder and Stoughton, London, p.133.

27 Mendonca, A.J. Boituka, Dahur Odi, Tiki o lé lé, O mai ita tebe, Makasae instruments, Personal communication, 2 February, 2011.

28 King, M. 1963, *Eden to Paradise*, Hodder and Stoughton, London, p.133.

29 Byrne, L. 1998, Tata-hateke ba dok: Grandfather Looking For The Future, CD, Tradisom records/Ministerio de Culturo, Portugal, p. 75.

30 Beloff, J. 1997, *The Ukulele: a visual history*, Miller Freeman Books, San Francisco.

31 Tingcai, W. 2010, <http://en.showchina.org/02/11/201008/t723955.html>

32 Byrne, L. 1998, *Tata-hateke ba dok: Grandfather Looking For The Future*, CD, Tradisom records/Ministerio de Culturo, Portugal, p. 75.

33 Mendonca, A.J. Boituka, Dahur Odi, Tiki o lé lé, O mai ita tebe, Makasae instruments, Personal communication, 2 February, 2011.

34 Mendonca, A.J. Boituka, Dahur Odi, Tiki o lé lé, O mai ita tebe, Makasae instruments, Personal communication, 2 February, 2011.

35 Mendonca, A.J. Boituka, Dahur Odi, Tiki o lé lé, O mai ita tebe, Makasae instruments, Personal communication, 2 February, 2011.

36 Gonçalves, O. Texts and meaning Fataluku songs, email, 3 June, 2011.

37 Lopes, L.S. 2010. Historia ikan Kelbeli, Personal communication, 17 July, 2010.

38 Sejismundu Pedro Valentim Ray, 2011, Personal Communication, October, 2011.

39 Sejismundu Pedro Valentim Ray, 2011, Personal Communication, October, 2011.

40 Sanches, A. Personal Communications, 25 September, 2011.

41 Gonçalves, O. Texts and meaning Fataluku songs, email, 3 June, 2011.

42 Sanches, A. Personal Communications, 25 September, 2011.

43 Daschbach, R. Personal paper: Music and Dance of Oekusi, Kutet, 20 May, 2011.

Axelson, E. 1973, *Portuguese in South-east Africa 1488-1600*, C.Struik, Johannesburg.

Barrkman, J. 2008, *Husi bei ala sira-nia liman : From the Hands of Our Ancestors: Arte no artesantu Timor-Leste : The Art and Craft of Timor-Leste*, Museum & Art Gallery, Northern Territory Darwin.

Barz, G. 2004, *Music In East Africa: Experiencing Music, Expressing Culture*, Oxford University Press, New York.

Bebey, F. 1975, *African Music: A People's Art*, George Harrap & Co, London.

Beloff, J. 1997, *The Ukulele: a visual history*, Miller Freeman Books, San Francisco.

Byrne, L. 1998, *Tata-hateke ba dok: Grandfather Looking For The Future*, CD, Tradisom records/Ministerio de Culturo, Portugal.

Byrne, L. 1998, 'Aman Ba Oan: getting inside the belly of the crocodile,' BArts [Hons] Thesis, Deakin University, Melbourne.

Cliff, M. 1984, *Timor: Legends and Poems from The Land of The Sleeping Crocodile*, H.C. Morris, Frankston.

Da Costa, D. Songs from Lolotoe, Personal Communication, 31 January, 2011.

Daschbach, R. Personal paper: Music and Dance of Oekusi, Kutet, 20 May, 2011.

Daschbach, R. *Pankalalàle*, meaning and lyrics, letter, 20 October, 2011.

Daschbach, R. Personal communication, 20 February, 2012.

De Silva J.S . 2008, *The Portuguese in - East Timor: A Cultural History of a Maritime Trading Empire*, Tauris Academic Studies, London.

England, N.M. 1995, *Music Among the Zul'was-si and Related Peoples of Namibia, Botswana, and Angola*, Harvard Dissertations in Folklore and oral Tradition, Garland Publishing, New York.

Flintoff, B. 2004, *Taonga Puoro: Singing Treasures*, Craig Potton Publishing, Nelson.

Forbes, H.O. 1885, *A Naturalist's Wanderings in the Eastern Archipelago: A narrative of Travel and Exploration from 1878 to 1883*, Samson Low, Marston, Searle, & Rivington, London.

Garfias, R. 2004, *The Bamboo Origins of far Eastern Bridged Zithers*, viewed 17 March 2011, <http://aris.ss.uci.edu/rgarfias/kiosk/chungkto.html>

Gomes, E.L. 2009, *Timor Leste Heartland: The Journey, Revolutionary Poems* (16 pieces),Melbourne. viewed 20 March, 2011, <http://timorlesteheartland.com/Poems.html>

Gonçalves, O. Texts and meaning Fatuluku songs, email, 3 June, 2011.

Gonçalves, O. & Adams, E. Semai Fatuluku song, email, 7 November, 2011.

Hastanto, S. 2007, *Asia-Pacific Database on Intangible Cultural Heritage: Performing Arts:Sasando*, viewed 21 April, 2011, <http://www.accu.or.jp/ich/en/arts/A_IDN9.html>

Hicks, D.1976, *Tetun Ghosts of Kin: Fieldwork in an Indonesian Community*, Mayfield Publishing, Palo Alto.

Hull, G. 2006, *Mai Kolia Tetun: A Beginner's Course in Tetum First National Language of East Timor*, 5th edn, Sebastiao Aparicio da Silva Project, Winston Hills.

Kartomi, M. 2000, *Music of Timor*, CD, Celestial Harmonies, Tucson.

Kartomi, M. 1985, *Musical Instruments of Indonesia: An Introductory Handbook*, Indonesian Arts Society, Melbourne.

Kartomi, M. & Blum, S. 1993, *Australian Studies in the History, Philosophy and Social Studies of Music : Music-Cultures in Contact: convergences and collisions*, Currency Press, Sydney.

King, M. 1963, *Eden To Paradise*, Hodder and Stoughton, London.

King-Boyes, M. 2001, 'Gates of Memory', PhD Thesis, Flinders University, Adelaide.

Lopes, L.S. Historia ikan Kelbeli, Personal communication, 17 July, 2010.

Matusky, P. & Beng,T.S. 2004, *The Music of Malaysia: The classical, folk, and syncretic traditions*, Ashgate Publishing Ltd, Surrey.

Mendonca, A.J. Boituka, Dahur Odi, Tiki o lé lé, O mai ita tebe, Makasae instruments, Personal communication, 2 February, 2011.

Menzies, G. 2002, *1421, The year China Discovered the World*, Bantam Books, London.

Miller, T.E .& Williams, S. 2008, *The Garland Handbook of Southeast Asian Music*, Routledge NY 10016, Taylor & Francis group, New York.

O'Connor, S. & Veth, P. 2000, *East of Wallace's Line: Studies of past and present maritime cultures of the Indo-pacific region*, A. A Balkema, Rotterdam.

Pereira, M. Lakadou, information, Personal communication, 16 April, 2004.

Ray, S.P. Tebe Makili, information, Personal communication, 9 October, 2011.

Sanches, A. Tupukur ulute, Vetere, Personal communication, 27 September, 2011.

Sarmento, E. Information on Mythology, instruments, Personal communication, 5 July, 2010.

Smith, V. Ailoos, Bidu Ailoos, Personal communications, 17 July, 2008.

Stone, R.M. 2005, *Music In West Africa, Experiencing Music, Expressing Culture*, Oxford University press, New York.

Taylor, J.G. 1999, *Politics in Contemporary Asia : East Timor: The Price of Freedom*, Pluto Press, Annandale.

Tingcai, W. 2010, Protection of Endangered Traditional Instrument, viewed 19 May, 2011, <http://en.showchina.org/02/11/201008/t723955.html>

Trindade, J. 2011, 'Lulik: The Core of Timorese Values,' paper presented at: Communicating New Research on Timor-Leste, third Timor-Leste Study Association Conference, Dili, East Timor, 30th June-1st July.

Traube, E. 1986, *Cosmology and Social Life: Ritual Exchange among the Mambai of East Timor*, University of Chicago Press, Chicago.

Wallace, A.R. 1869, *The Malay Archipelago: The land of the Orang-Utan, and the Bird of Paradise. A Narrative of Travel, with Studies of Man and Nature*, Macmillan & Co, London.

Yampolsky, P. 1998, *Music of Indonesia Vol. 16, Music from the Southeast: Sumbawa, Sumba, Timor*, CD, Smithsonian Folkways, Washington, DC.

Kréditu ba husi pintura sira
PICTURE CREDITS : PAINTINGS

3	*Together Will be Nice*	Avelino Jose Cancio da Silva
20	*Scape of Dili Beach*	Pelle Pereira
23	*Abo Ferik*	Cesar Augusto Soares Lourdes
26	*Danca Lensun*	Benvindo Ximenes Fraya
31	*East Timor Woman*	Vicente Soares
38	*Makikit*	Grinaldo Gilmarodep Fernandes
42	*Bidu*	Jemito Antonio Alves
46	*Cultura Rai Nain*	Januario Gueterres Parada
50	*Lakadou 1*	Cesar Augusto Soares Lourdes
54	*Dance for Better Times*	Alfeo Sanches Pereira
56	*Mane-oan Oekusi*	Alfeo Sanches Pereira
58	*Katuas Oekusi*	Cesar Augusto Soares Lourdes
78	*Ferik ho Tala*	Arsenio Jekonia
84	*Tutuala*	Tony Amaral
95	*Titir*	Cesar Augusto Soares Lourdes
102	*Manu*	Pavao Silvia
122	*Ba Futura*	Natalino Dos Reis Pires
140	*Don't Kick Us*	Jose Amaral
148	*Lakadou 2*	Cesar Augusto Soares Lourdes

Kréditu ba fotografia
PICTURE CREDITS : PHOTOGRAPHS

8	*Mountain - Ainaro*	Ros Dunlop
11	*Ros Dunlop with family of Ameta Jorges Ximenes Mendonca - Baukau*	Penelope Lee
18	*Area Branca - Dili*	Penelope Lee
28	*Likurai dancers - Kovalima*	Charline Bodin
	Masked dancers, Luro, Lautein	Margaret King 1963
29	*Likurai dancers - Suai Loro*	Charline Bodin
	Katuas - Mulo	Ros Dunlop
30	*Katuas - Mulo*	Ros Dunlop
	Dancer in traditional dress - Suai Loro	Ros Dunlop
	Musician (Joao Baro) in traditional dress - Suai Loro	Ros Dunlop
	Dancer in traditional dress - Suai Loro	Ros Dunlop
	Dancer in traditional dress, Grupu Rebenta - Bacau	Penelope Lee
	Manu fulun & kaebauk	Ros Dunlop
	Kaebauk	Ros Dunlop
31	*Belak*	John Lee
	Morteen	John Lee
32	*Villagers dancing the dahur - Manoloon*	Ros Dunlop
33	*Dancers, Grupu Rebenta - Baukau*	Penelope Lee
34	*Likurai dancers - Kovalima*	Charline Bodin
35	*Bidu tais mutin - Suai Loro*	Ros Dunlop
	Ailoos musicians, Grupu Lafaek - Suai Loro	Ros Dunlop

36	*Dahur - Blaro* Ros Dunlop
	Dancers, Grupu Rebenta - Baukau Ros Dunlop
37	*Likurai - Suai Loro* Charline Bodin
	Grupu Lafaek - Suai Loro Ros Dunlop
39	*Katuas - Mulo* Ros Dunlop
40	*Dancers, Grupu Lafaek - Suai Loro* Ros Dunlop
41	*Katuas in front of Uma Lulik - Mulo* Ros Dunlop
43	*Snared baba dook* Ros Dunlop
44	*Tala - Mulo* Ros Dunlop
45	*Aíloos musicians, Grupu Lafaek - Suai Loro* Ros Dunlop
47	*Ferik playing baba dook* Bernadino Soares
48	*Baba dook* Ros Dunlop
49	*Raraun musician (Joao Baros) - Suai Loro* Ros Dunlop
51	*Lakadou* Ros Dunlop
52	*Lakadou* Ros Dunlop
53	*Manuel Pereira playing Lakadou* Ros Dunlop
	Lakadou musicians - Gleno Ros Dunlop
59	*Takanab - Baki* Don Bennetts
60	*Oekusi dancer in traditional dress - Baki* Don Bennetts
61	*Bonet - Baki* Ros Dunlop
62	*Oekusi dancer in traditional dress - Baki* Don Bennetts
63	*Bsoot dancers - Baki* Ros Dunlop
64	*Bano* Ros Dunlop
65	*Babuk* Ros Dunlop
	Bano Ros Dunlop
	Bano Don Bennetts
66	*Bsoot, Topu Honis - Kuket* Ros Dunlop
68	*Ke'e* Ros Dunlop
	Tala Penelope Lee
69	*Musicians playing sene and tala - Kutet* Ros Dunlop
70	*Bonet, Topu Honis - Kutet* Don Bennetts
73	*Bonet, Topu Honis - Kutet* Don Bennetts
75	*Pankalalále - Kutet* Ros Dunlop
77	*Garden and woman gardening - Kutet* Ros Dunlop
80	*Mountains - Oekusi* Ros Dunlop
81	*Central Mountain Range* Ros Dunlop
83	*Women singing Oebani - Kutet* Ros Dunlop
86	*Uma Lulik - Iliomar* Ros Dunlop
88	*Katuas playing karau dikur - Mulo* Ros Dunlop
89	*Kokotere mouthpiece - Venilalae* Alfeo Sanches
	Armando de Jesus, kokotere player - Venilalae Alfeo Sanches
90	*Karau dikur - Mulo* Ros Dunlop
91	*Kokotere bell* Alfeo Sanches
92	*Tohin & tala - Blaro* Ros Dunlop
93	*Katuas playing tohin - Blaro* Ros Dunlop
	Katuas playing tohin beside a tara bandu - Mulo Ros Dunlop
94	*Tihak - Makili* Ros Dunlop
	Paulino Ximenes with tihak - Makili Ros Dunlop
96	*Titir* Margaret King 1963
97	*Titir - Iliomar* Ros Dunlop
	Bobakasa Ros Dunlop
98	*Tohin - Mulo* Ros Dunlop
99	*Tihak - Makili* Ros Dunlop
100	*Ameta Jorges Ximenes Mendonca playing bobakasa and tightening the bobakasa - Baukau* Penelope Lee
	Bobakasa - Baukau Penelope Lee
104	*Rice paddies, road to Venilale* Penelope Lee
105	*Pig/fahi* Penelope Lee
106	*Kakal'uta* Ros Dunlop
107	*Kakalo - Los Palos* Tony Hicks
108	*Kakalo - Los Palos* Tony Hicks
109	*Kakal'uta - Los Palos* Ros Dunlop
110	*Marco Amaral da Silva playing Kafu'i - Ossu* Ros Dunlop
111	*Four kafu'i* Ros Dunlop
	Lesun no alu - Kamanasa Ros Dunlop
112	*Kafu'i with machete - Gildapil* Ros Dunlop
	Kafu'i with carving Ros Dunlop
113	*Mouthpiece detail of kafu'i - Ossu* Ros Dunlop
	Kafu'i players - Gildapil Penelope Lee
	Albilio Soares Rai Gua playing kafu'i boot - Likisa Ros Dunlop
114	*Clemente Forces playing rama - Makadade* Sejismundo Pedro Valentim Ray
	Rama detail Sejismundo Pedro Valentim Ray
115	*Clemente Forces playing rama* Sejismundo Pedro Valentim Ray
116	*Kakeit* Ros Dunlop
117	*Three details of bijol meto* Ros Dunlop
118	*Clemente Forces playing kakeit - Makadade* Sejismundo Pedro Valentim Ray
119	*Three details of bijol meto* Ros Dunlop
120	*Jaineito Pereira De Aroujo playing au - Likisá* Ros Dunlop
124	*Grupu Rebenta - Baukau* Cesario Soares Lourdes
127	*Grupu Rebenta - Baukau* Cesario Soares Lourdes
128	*Grupu Rebenta - Baukau* Penelope Lee
132	*Katuas - Mulo* Ros Dunlop
135	*Fish carving in house of Max Stahl* Penelope Lee
	Beach scene - Ataúru Ros Dunlop
136	*Fatuk Kelbeli, the sacred rock used in the ceremony for the hunting of Kelbeli - Dair* Ros Dunlop
	Special boat (Ese-Mau Mekei) used in the ceremony for the hunting of Kelbeli, pulled by villagers of Dair Ros Dunlop
137	*Beach scene - Ataúru* Ros Dunlop
142	*Etson Caminha and son - Dili* Ros Dunlop
143	*Girls from Balibo* Ros Dunlop
147	*Beach Scene - Jako Island* Ros Dunlop
151	*Mountain landscape - Ainaro* Ros Dunlop

Background tais and weaving from the collections of Ros Dunlop and Jenni Kanaley John Lee